# AQA GCSE (9–1) English Literature

# The Strange Case of Dr Jekyll and Mr Hyde

Emma Clark

Published by Pearson Education Limited, 80 Strand, London, WC2R 0RL.
www.pearsonschoolsandfecolleges.co.uk

Text © Pearson Education Ltd 2018
Produced and typeset by QBS Learning

The right of Emma Clark to be identified as author of this work has been asserted by her in accordance with the Copyright, Designs and Patents Act 1988.

First published 2018

21 20 19 18
10 9 8 7 6 5 4 3 2 1

**British Library Cataloguing in Publication Data**
A catalogue record for this book is available from the British Library

ISBN 978 1 292 25079 3

**Copyright notice**
All rights reserved. No part of this publication may be reproduced in any form or by any means (including photocopying or storing it in any medium by electronic means and whether or not transiently or incidentally to some other use of this publication) without the written permission of the copyright owner, except in accordance with the provisions of the Copyright, Designs and Patents Act 1988 or under the terms of a licence issued by the Copyright Licensing Agency, Barnard's Inn, 86 Fetter Lane, London EC4A 1EN (www.cla.co.uk). Applications for the copyright owner's written permission should be addressed to the publisher.

Printed in Slovakia by Neografia

**Note from the publisher**
Pearson has robust editorial processes, including answer and fact checks, to ensure the accuracy of the content in this publication, and every effort is made to ensure this publication is free of errors. We are, however, only human, and occasionally errors do occur. Pearson is not liable for any misunderstandings that arise as a result of errors in this publication, but it is our priority to ensure that the content is accurate. If you spot an error, please do contact us at resourcescorrections@pearson.com so we can make sure it is corrected.

# Contents

## 1 Getting the plot straight
Get started — 1
1. How do I make sure I know the plot? — 3
2. How can I explore the development of the plot? — 4
3. How do I know which are the most significant events in the novel? — 5
Get back on track — 6

## 2 Analysing the extract
Get started — 9
1. How do I choose the points I need to make? — 11
2. How do I develop my analysis? — 12
3. How do I structure a paragraph of analysis? — 13
Get back on track — 14

## 3 Commenting on the writer's choices in the extract
Get started — 17
1. How do I identify significant language choices? — 19
2. How do I identify significant sentence forms and structural choices? — 20
3. How do I comment on the writer's choices? — 21
Get back on track — 22

## 4 Exploring themes and characters
Get started — 25
1. How do I track the development of a character? — 27
2. How do I explore a theme? — 28
3. How do I comment on the development of character or theme? — 29
Get back on track — 30

## 5 Planning your response
Get started — 33
1. How do I make a critical judgement? — 35
2. How do I gather relevant points? — 36
3. How do I sequence my points? — 37
Get back on track — 38

## 6 Writing your response
Get started — 41
1. How do I choose key events and key quotations to learn? — 43
2. How do I use evidence to support my ideas? — 44
3. How do I analyse my evidence? — 45
Get back on track — 46

## 7 Commenting on structure
Get started — 49
1. How can I comment on the settings in the novel? — 51
2. How can I comment on the structure of the novel? — 52
3. How do I analyse the writer's use of structure? — 53
Get back on track — 54

## 8 Commenting on context
Get started — 57
1. How do I know which contextual ideas to write about? — 59
2. How do I comment on context? — 60
3. How do I build my comments on context into my analysis? — 61
Get back on track — 62

## 9 Developing a critical writing style
Get started — 65
1. How do I choose vocabulary that expresses my ideas precisely? — 67
2. How can I link my ideas to express them more clearly? — 68
3. How can I extend my sentences to develop my ideas more fully? — 69
Get back on track — 70

**More practice questions** — 73

**Answers** — 78

**Get started**    Read, understand and respond to texts (AO1)

# 1 Getting the plot straight

This unit will help you to understand and remember the plot of *The Strange Case of Dr Jekyll and Mr Hyde*. The skills you will build are to:

- remember the sequence of key events in the novel
- understand the causes and consequences of the key events in the novel
- understand what makes some events in the novel more significant than others.

In the exam you will face questions like the one below. This is about the extract on the next page. At the end of the unit you will **plan your own response** to this question.

> **Exam-style question**
>
> Starting with this extract, how does Stevenson present the importance of relationships in *The Strange Case of Dr Jekyll and Mr Hyde*?
>
> Write about:
> - how Stevenson presents the importance of relationships in this extract
> - how Stevenson presents the importance of relationships in the novel as a whole.
>
> (30 marks)

Before you tackle the question you will work through three key questions in the **skills boosts** to help you to get the plot of *The Strange Case of Dr Jekyll and Mr Hyde* straight.

| 1. How do I make sure I know the plot? | 2. How can I explore the development of the plot? | 3. How do I know which are the most significant events in the novel? |

Read the extract on the next page from Chapter 2 of *The Strange Case of Dr Jekyll and Mr Hyde*.

**As you read, think about the following:**

 Where in the novel does this extract appear? Is it near the beginning, in the middle or at the end?

 What has happened before this extract? What happens after this extract?

 In what ways does Stevenson present friendship in the extract?

Unit 1 Getting the plot straight      1

# Get started

> **Exam-style question**
>
> Read the following extract from Chapter 2 of *The Strange Case of Dr Jekyll and Mr Hyde*.
>
> At this point in the novel, Mr Utterson and Dr Lanyon are talking about their friend, Dr Jekyll.

### Extract A | Chapter 2 of *The Strange Case of Dr Jekyll and Mr Hyde*

The solemn butler knew and welcomed him; he was subjected to no stage of delay, but ushered direct from the door to the dining-room where Dr Lanyon sat alone over his wine. This was a hearty, healthy, dapper, red-faced gentleman, with a shock of hair prematurely white, and a boisterous and decided manner. At sight of Mr Utterson, he sprang up from his chair and welcomed him with both hands. The geniality, as was the way of the man, was
5  somewhat theatrical to the eye; but it reposed on genuine feeling. For these two were old friends, old mates both at school and college, both thorough respectors of themselves and of each other, and what does not always follow, men who thoroughly enjoyed each other's company.
After a little rambling talk, the lawyer led up to the subject which so disagreeably preoccupied his mind.
'I suppose, Lanyon,' said he, 'you and I must be the two oldest friends that Henry Jekyll has?'
10  'I wish the friends were younger,' chuckled Dr Lanyon. 'But I suppose we are. And what of that? I see little of him now.'
'Indeed?' said Utterson. 'I thought you had a bond of common interest.'
'We had,' was the reply. 'But it is more than ten years since Henry Jekyll became too fanciful for me. He began to go wrong, wrong in mind; and though of course I continue to take an interest in him for old sake's sake, as they say, I
15  see and I have seen devilish little of the man. Such unscientific balderdash,' added the doctor, flushing suddenly purple, 'would have estranged Damon and Pythias.'

**2   Unit 1 Getting the plot straight**

## Skills boost

### 1 How do I make sure I know the plot?

*The Strange Case of Dr Jekyll and Mr Hyde* is written in 10 chapters. Focus on the memorable key characters and events that appear in each chapter to make sure you know the novel's plot.

1. The accounts of Mr Hyde's violent attacks on people are key events in the novel.

   a. Circle  how many times Mr Hyde attacks someone.

   | 1 | 2 | 3 | 4 | 5 |

   b. In which chapter does each attack appear? Add ✎ this information to the plot summary below.

2. What happens at the beginning and the end of the novel? Add ✎ the key events to the plot summary below.

Plot summary

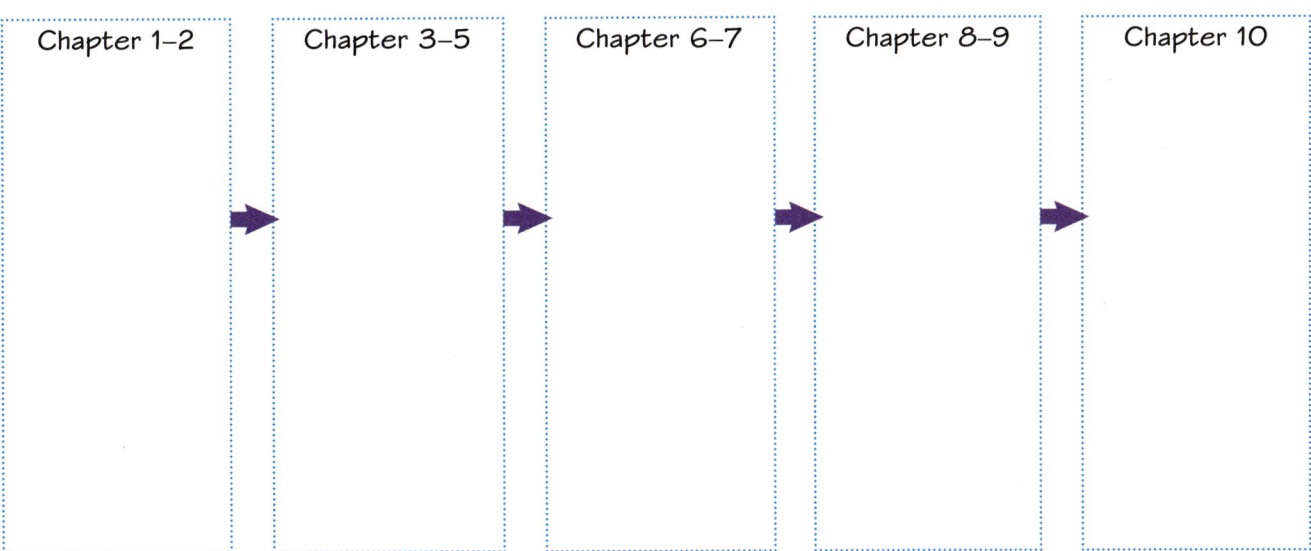

| Chapter 1–2 | Chapter 3–5 | Chapter 6–7 | Chapter 8–9 | Chapter 10 |

3. The reader is introduced to some characters in detail who are important throughout the novel, and others who feature in a key event. (The remaining characters are not significant.)

   a. Label ✎ the characters listed below with 'D' if they are detailed and 'K' if they only feature in a key event.

   b. Add ✎ each character, and any other details about what they do or say, to the plot summary above.

   > Some characters may appear more than once. Check you have added these characters to every key event in which they appear.

| | | |
|---|---|---|
| Mr Richard Enfield (Mr Utterson's friend and cousin) ☐ | Mr Gabriel Utterson (a lawyer) ☐ | Dr Henry Jekyll (a respected doctor) ☐ |
| Dr Hastie Lanyon (a doctor) ☐ | Mr Poole (a butler) ☐ | Mr Edward Hyde (the alter ego of Jekyll) ☐ |
| The maid ☐ | Inspector Newcomen ☐ | Mr Guest (Utterson's clerk) ☐ |
| Sir Danvers Carew (an MP) ☐ | Mr Hyde's landlady ☐ | Bradshaw ☐ |

**Unit 1 Getting the plot straight**  3

## Skills boost

### 2 How can I explore the development of the plot?

The plot of *The Strange Case of Dr Jekyll and Mr Hyde* follows the events surrounding the mysterious Mr Hyde and the eventual death of Dr Jekyll.

 Look at some of the key events in the plot of this novel.

**Chapter 1**
- Mr Utterson and his friend Mr Enfield see a worn doorway.
- The door reminds Enfield of a man, Mr Hyde, whom he saw trampling over a girl. He later saw Hyde enter this door, which is at the back of Jekyll's house.

**Chapter 2**
- Utterson reads Dr Jekyll's will, which states that he wants to leave Hyde all his money if he dies or goes missing.
- Utterson meets Hyde near the same door and finds him very unnerving.

**Chapter 3**
- Utterson talks to Jekyll about his will and Hyde. Jekyll refuses to discuss it.

**Chapter 4**
- A year later, Hyde is witnessed murdering Sir Danvers Carew, an MP.
- The police find a letter addressed to Utterson on Carew's body.
- Utterson and the police go to Hyde's house, but he is not there. They find half the walking stick that was used to kill Carew.

**Chapter 5**
- Utterson visits an ill Jekyll, who gives him a letter written by Hyde.
- Hyde's and Jekyll's handwriting is found to be very similar.

**Chapter 6**
- Lanyon falls ill after a terrible shock and dies, leaving a letter for Utterson to read if Jekyll goes missing or dies.

**Chapter 7**
- Enfield and Utterson see an ill Jekyll at the window; he turns away from them.

**Chapter 8**
- Poole asks Utterson to help him break into Jekyll's laboratory, where they discover Hyde, who has killed himself with poison.
- There is no sign of Jekyll, but they find a long statement written by him, and a new will, in which he leaves all his money to Utterson.

**Chapter 9**
- Lanyon recounts, in a letter, how Hyde turned into Jekyll in front of him after drinking a potion.

**Chapter 10**
- Jekyll explains in his statement that transforming into Hyde allowed him to live a double life, and how it would lead to his death.

a Underline (A) the key events that allow us to learn more about the character of Mr Hyde.

b Circle (A) any key events that suggest Dr Jekyll is Mr Hyde.

**4 Unit 1 Getting the plot straight**

## Skills boost

### 3 How do I know which are the most significant events in the novel?

Understanding what each key event in the novel contributes to the plot will help you to get the plot straight and identify significant parts of the novel to write about in your responses.

Look at some of the key events in the plot of *The Strange Case of Dr Jekyll and Mr Hyde*.

**Chapter 1**
- Mr Utterson and his friend Mr Enfield see a worn doorway.
- The door reminds Enfield of a man, Mr Hyde, whom he saw trampling over a girl. He later saw Hyde enter this door, which is at the back of Jekyll's house.

**Chapter 2**
- Utterson reads Dr Jekyll's will, which states that he wants to leave Hyde all his money if he dies or goes missing.
- Utterson meets Hyde near the same door and finds him very unnerving.

**Chapter 3**
- Utterson talks to Jekyll about his will and Hyde. Jekyll refuses to discuss it.

**Chapter 4**
- A year later, Hyde is witnessed murdering Sir Danvers Carew, an MP.
- The police find a letter addressed to Utterson on Carew's body.
- Utterson and the police go to Hyde's house, but he is not there. They find half the walking stick that was used to kill Carew.

**Chapter 5**
- Utterson visits an ill Jekyll, who gives him a letter written by Hyde.
- Hyde's and Jekyll's handwriting is found to be very similar.

**Chapter 6**
- Lanyon falls ill after a terrible shock and dies, leaving a letter for Utterson to read if Jekyll goes missing or dies.

**Chapter 7**
- Enfield and Utterson see an ill Jekyll at the window; he turns away from them.

**Chapter 8**
- Poole asks Utterson to help him break into Jekyll's laboratory, where they discover Hyde, who has killed himself with poison.
- There is no sign of Jekyll, but they find a long statement written by him, and a new will, in which he leaves all his money to Utterson.

**Chapter 9**
- Lanyon recounts, in a letter, how Hyde turned into Jekyll in front of him after drinking a potion.

**Chapter 10**
- Jekyll explains in his statement that transforming into Hyde allowed him to live a double life, and how it would lead to his death.

(1) Circle (A) the key events above that mention documents such as letters and wills.

(2) a  For each key point, ask yourself: How significant is it to the story? Then give ✏️ each one a mark out of ten: 1/10 = not at all significant; 10/10 = highly significant.

   b  Tick ✓ the three events you have marked the highest.

**Unit 1 Getting the plot straight** 5

### Get back on track

# Getting the plot straight

To plan and write an effective response about *The Strange Case of Dr Jekyll and Mr Hyde*, you need to:
- know the key events in each chapter of the novel and the order in which they happen
- understand what each event in the plot contributes to the story
- be able to identify the most significant events in the novel and explain their significance.

Look again at the **first** part of the exam-style question you saw at the start of the unit.

**Exam-style question**

Starting with this extract, how does Stevenson present the importance of relationships?

Write about:
- how Stevenson presents the importance of relationships in this extract.

**(1)** Now look at one student's planning notes, written in response to this exam-style question.

*Before this extract:* We meet Utterson. He and Enfield are friends but have little in common. Enfield tells him about Hyde and the girl, which reminds Utterson of Jekyll and his will.

*After this extract:* Utterson supports Jekyll and receives letters from both Lanyon and Jekyll which lead him to the truth about Hyde.

So in Chapter 2, the relationship is important, as it introduces us to Hyde through the conversation of the two friends.

*In the extract:*
- The relationship is close – Lanyon welcomes Utterson with 'both hands'.
- The two men went to school together and not only know each other but 'enjoyed each other's company'.
- Difference highlighted between their relationship and Lanyon's friendship with Jekyll. Lanyon admits he has not seen him for 'more than ten years' due to Jekyll's 'unscientific balderdash' – introduces the idea of Jekyll's unconventional ideas about science.

- Shows awareness of **where** in the novel the extract is taken from
- Makes a clear, direct **response** to the question
- Uses **key words** from the question
- Makes a **range of points**
- Supports points with **evidence**
- **Comments** on the significance of the writer's choices

Look carefully at the annotations above showing what makes a successful response. Draw lines linking each annotation to a relevant part of the student's plan, to show how the plan will help to make their response to the first part of the question above successful.

**6** Unit 1 Getting the plot straight

# Your turn!

**Get back on track**

You are now going to **write your own answer** in response to the exam-style question.

### Exam-style question

Starting with this extract, how does Stevenson present the importance of relationships?

Write about:
- how Stevenson presents the importance of relationships in this extract
- how Stevenson presents the importance of relationships in the novel as a whole.

**1** Look again at some of the key events in the novel.    ✗  ✓

| | |
|---|---|
| **Chapter 1** | Mr Utterson and his friend Mr Enfield see a worn doorway. |
| | The door reminds Enfield of a man, Mr Hyde, whom he saw trampling over a girl. He later saw Hyde enter this door, which is at the back of Jekyll's house. |
| **Chapter 2** | Utterson reads Dr Jekyll's will, which states that he wants to leave Hyde all his money if he dies or goes missing. |
| | Utterson meets Hyde near the same door and finds him very unnerving. |
| **Chapter 3** | Utterson talks to Jekyll about his will and Hyde. Jekyll refuses to discuss it. |
| **Chapter 4** | A year later, Hyde is witnessed murdering Sir Danvers Carew, an MP. |
| | The police find a letter addressed to Utterson on Carew's body. |
| | Utterson and the police go to Hyde's house, but he is not there. They find half the walking stick that was used to kill Carew. |
| **Chapter 5** | Utterson visits an ill Jekyll, who gives him a letter written by Hyde. |
| | Hyde's and Jekyll's handwriting is found to be very similar. |
| **Chapter 6** | Lanyon falls ill after a terrible shock and dies, leaving a letter for Utterson to read if Jekyll goes missing or dies. |
| **Chapter 7** | Enfield and Utterson see an ill Jekyll at the window; he turns away from them. |
| **Chapter 8** | Poole asks Utterson to help him break into Jekyll's laboratory, where they discover Hyde, who has killed himself with poison. |
| | There is no sign of Jekyll, but they find a long statement written by him, and a new will, in which he leaves all his money to Utterson. |
| **Chapter 9** | Lanyon recounts, in a letter, how Hyde turned into Jekyll in front of him after drinking a potion. |
| **Chapter 10** | Jekyll explains in his statement that transforming into Hyde allowed him to live a double life, and how it would lead to his death. |

**a** Which key events show different relationships? Tick ✓ them.

**b** Which of these events show the **importance** of relationships? Cross ✗ them.

**Unit 1 Getting the plot straight**

# Review your skills

## Check up

Review your response for the exam-style question on page 7. Tick ✓ the column to show how well you think you have done each of the following.

|  | Not quite ✓ | Nearly there ✓ | Got it! ✓ |
|---|---|---|---|
| identified key events in the story that show the main relationships in the novel | ☐ | ☐ | ☐ |
| identified key events in the story that show the differing relationships in the novel | ☐ | ☐ | ☐ |
| identified key events in the story that show the **importance** of relationships in the novel | ☐ | ☐ | ☐ |

Look over all of your work in this unit. Note down ✎ the **three** most important things to remember when selecting key events for a question about *The Strange Case of Dr Jekyll and Mr Hyde*.

1. ................................................................................
2. ................................................................................
3. ................................................................................

## Need more practice?

Here is another exam-style question, this time relating to the extract from Chapter 2 on page 73 (Extract A).

### Exam-style question

Starting with this extract, how does Stevenson present Utterson in *The Strange Case of Dr Jekyll and Mr Hyde*?

Write about:

- how Stevenson presents Utterson in this extract
- how Stevenson presents Utterson in the novel as a whole.

(30 marks)

Which key events in the novel would you choose to write ✎ about in your response to this question?

How confident do you feel about each of these **skills**? Colour ✎ in the bars.

**1** How do I make sure I know the plot?

**2** How can I explore the development of the plot?

**3** How do I know which are the most significant events in the novel?

8   Unit 1 Getting the plot straight

 **Get started**    Read, understand and respond to texts (AO1)

# ② Analysing the extract

This unit will help you to explore the extract in the first part of the exam question on *The Strange Case of Dr Jekyll and Mr Hyde*. The skills you will build are to:
- select relevant points to make in your analysis of the extract
- develop your analysis
- structure your analysis.

In the exam you will face questions like the one below. This is about the extract on the next page. At the end of the unit you will **write one paragraph** in response to this question, **focusing on the extract**.

> **Exam-style question**
>
> Starting with this extract, how does Stevenson present Mr Hyde as evil and menacing?
>
> Write about:
> - how Stevenson presents Mr Hyde in this extract
> - how Stevenson presents Mr Hyde as evil and menacing in the novel as a whole.
>
> (30 marks)

Before you tackle the question you will work through three key questions in the **skills boosts** to help you analyse the extract.

① **How do I choose the points I need to make?**    ② **How do I develop my analysis?**    ③ **How do I structure a paragraph of analysis?**

Read the extract on the next page from Chapter 1 of *The Strange Case of Dr Jekyll and Mr Hyde*.

### As you read, think about the following:

 What has happened before this extract? What happens after this extract?

 How does Stevenson present the reactions of Mr Hyde in this extract?

 How does Stevenson present the actions of Mr Hyde in this extract?

Unit 2 Analysing the extract    9

## Get started

**Exam-style question**

Read the following extract from Chapter 1 of *The Strange Case of Dr Jekyll and Mr Hyde*.

At this point in the novel, Mr Enfield recounts a violent incident involving Mr Hyde and a young girl.

**Extract A** | Chapter 1 of *The Strange Case of Dr Jekyll and Mr Hyde*

All at once, I saw two figures: one a little man who was stumping along eastward at a good walk, and the other a girl of maybe eight or ten who was running as hard as she was able down a cross street. Well, sir, the two ran into one another naturally enough at the corner; and then came the horrible part of the thing; for the man trampled calmly over the child's body and left her screaming on the ground. It sounds nothing to hear, but it was hellish to
5  see. It wasn't like a man; it was like some damned **Juggernaut**. I gave a few halloa, took to my heels, collared my gentleman, and brought him back to where there was already quite a group about the screaming child. He was perfectly cool and made no resistance, but gave me one look, so ugly that it brought out the sweat on me like running. The people who had turned out were the girl's own family; and pretty soon, the doctor, for whom she had been sent, put in his appearance. Well, the child was not much the worse, more frightened, according to the
10  Sawbones; and there you might have supposed would be an end to it. But there was one curious circumstance. I had taken a loathing to my gentleman at first sight. So had the child's family, which was only natural. But the doctor's case was what struck me. He was the usual cut and dry apothecary, of no particular age and colour, with a strong Edinburgh accent and about as emotional as a bagpipe. Well, sir, he was like the rest of us; every time he looked at my prisoner, I saw that Sawbones turn sick and white with the desire to kill him. I knew what was in his
15  mind, just as he knew what was in mine; and killing being out of the question, we did the next best. We told the man we could and would make such a scandal out of this as should make his name stink from one end of London to the other. If he had any friends or any credit, we undertook that he should lose them. And all the time, as we were pitching it in red hot, we were keeping the women off him as best we could for they were as wild as harpies. I never saw a circle of such hateful faces; and there was the man in the middle, with a kind of black sneering
20  coolness – frightened too, I could see that – but carrying it off, sir, really like Satan.

*Juggernaut:* A force destroying everything in its path named after the chariot of the Hindu god, Jagannatha.

10   Unit 2 Analysing the extract

## Skills boost

###  How do I choose the points I need to make?

The first thing you need to do is to identify which parts of the extract you can explore further in your response to the question.

Look again at the exam-style question you are exploring.

**Exam-style question**

Starting with this extract, how does Stevenson present Mr Hyde as evil and menacing?

(1) Now look through the extract on page 10, focusing on each section in turn:

| 1 | Mr Enfield sees a man and a young girl running in opposite directions and describes how they collide. [lines 1–3] |
| 2 | The man 'trampled calmly' over the girl like a 'Juggernaut'. [lines 3–5] |
| 3 | Enfield catches the man and brings him back to the crowd. [lines 5–6] |
| 4 | Mr Hyde puts up no resistance and says nothing. [lines 6–7] |
| 5 | Enfield and the doctor both take a dislike to Mr Hyde. [lines 11–14] |
| 6 | Enfield threatens Mr Hyde with a scandal; he reacts with a 'black sneering coolness'. [lines 15–20] |

a. Decide which **three** sections reveal most about how Stevenson presents Mr Hyde as evil and menacing. Label them A, B and C.

**Think about:**
- Enfield's description of the incident between Mr Hyde and the girl
- the description of Mr Hyde's reactions after the incident.

b. Note below what each of the sections you have chosen reveals about how Stevenson presents Mr Hyde as evil and menacing.

A

B

C

Unit 2 Analysing the extract

## Skills boost

### 2. How do I develop my analysis?

To develop your analysis, you need to think about how the characters, events or setting are described in the extract, and what this reveals about the aspect of the novel you are exploring. Your ideas need to be supported by evidence from the extract.

Look again at the exam-style question you are exploring.

**Exam-style question**

Starting with this extract, how does Stevenson present Mr Hyde as evil and menacing?

**1** Now look at one section from the extract that reveals something about Mr Hyde:

> All at once, I saw two figures: one a little man who was stumping along eastward at a good walk, and the other a girl of maybe eight or ten who was running as hard as she was able down a cross street. Well, sir, the two ran into one another naturally enough at the corner; and then came the horrible part of the thing; for the man trampled calmly over the child's body and left her screaming on the ground. It sounds nothing to hear, but it was hellish to see. It wasn't like a man; it was like some damned Juggernaut.

**a** Write a few words in the space above that sum up your impression of Mr Hyde from this description.

*Look for all the words and phrases used to describe Hyde and his actions.*

**b** Why might Stevenson have chosen to describe Mr Hyde in this way? Write one or two sentences explaining your ideas.

..................................................................................................
..................................................................................................
..................................................................................................

**c** Look again at your answers above. How does this description of Mr Hyde's actions help to show him as evil and menacing?

..................................................................................................
..................................................................................................
..................................................................................................

**d** Which parts of the description show this most clearly? Choose **two** short quotations and underline Ⓐ them with one line.

**2 a** Choose another section from the extract on page 10 that shows Mr Hyde as evil and menacing. Circle Ⓐ the section and then annotate it, noting down:
- the impression the section creates
- how it helps to show Mr Hyde as evil and menacing.

**b** Now double underline Ⓐ **two** short quotations to support your ideas.

Unit 2 Analysing the extract

## Skills boost

### 3. How do I structure a paragraph of analysis?

Each paragraph of your analysis should include:
- a key point focusing on the key words in the question
- evidence from the text to support your point
- comments on the evidence and its impact
- a summary of your response to the question.

You can structure these four elements in different ways.

> For more on detailed analysis of the writer's choices in the extract, see Unit 3.

Look at the sentences from one paragraph of a student's response to this exam-style question.

**Exam-style question**

Starting with this extract, how does Stevenson present Mr Hyde as evil and menacing?

| | |
|---|---|
| A | The description of Mr Hyde walking over the girl and not looking back develops the reader's impression that he is evil and menacing. |
| B | We are told that he 'trampled over the child's body' and then he left her 'screaming on the ground'. |
| C | Stevenson describes how Hyde 'wasn't like a man' but like a 'Juggernaut', indicating that he is menacing. |
| D | The reactions of others underline his menacing nature, as when Enfield takes a 'loathing' to him, and the look Hyde gives him is so 'ugly' that it makes him sweat. |
| E | Instead of being sorry, Hyde is cold and calm at all times. |
| F | Hyde is evil and not like other people. |

**1**
  **a** Which of these sentences would you include in a paragraph in your response to the exam-style question above? Tick ✓ them.
  **b** How would you sequence your chosen sentences in a paragraph? Number them.

**2** To make your paragraph even more effective, look at some of the linking phrases below (or use your own) and add them to your chosen sentences above.

| In this way, | Similarly, | This suggests that | For example, | It implies that |

**3** Look again at the sentences you have chosen and sequenced.
  **a** Which sentences make a key point? Label them **KP** (key point).
  **b** Which support a key point using evidence? Label them **E** (evidence).
  **c** Which comment on the evidence and its impact? Label them **C** (comment).
  **d** Which show a response to the question? Label them **R** (response).

Unit 2 Analysing the extract

Get back on track

# Analysing the extract

To analyse the extract effectively, you need to:
- identify the parts of the extract that are relevant to the question
- explore what these parts suggest about the focus of the question
- structure your paragraphs of analysis to include a key point supported by evidence, a comment on its impact and a response to the question.

Look at the exam-style question you saw at the start of the unit.

**Exam-style question**

Starting with this extract, how does Stevenson present Mr Hyde as evil and menacing in *The Strange Tale of Dr Jekyll and Mr Hyde*?

**1** Look at this paragraph, taken from a student's response to this question. It focuses on the extract on page 10.

> In this extract, Mr Hyde is clearly shown as evil and menacing. His actions make this clear to the reader when we are told that he 'calmly trampled over the child's body and left her screaming on the ground'. This description of Hyde as 'calm' implies that Hyde did not care about the screaming girl, which makes him an evil character. This is further underlined when Enfield says Hyde gave him 'one look, so ugly' that it brought him out in a sweat 'like running'. The impression created by this sentence is that Hyde is so menacing he causes other people to be nervous and feel uncomfortable.

**a** Which of the following has this student achieved? Tick ✓ them.

A Identified parts of the extract that are relevant to the question.

B Made a key point.

C Supported it with evidence.

D Commented on its impact.

E Responded to the question.

**b** Highlight and label ✏ where in the paragraph this student has achieved A–E.

14   Unit 2 Analysing the extract

**Get back on track**

# Your turn!

You are now going to write **one or two paragraphs** in response to the exam-style question below, **focusing on these sections** of the extract on page 10.

**1**
I had taken a loathing to my gentleman at first sight. So had the child's family, which was only natural. But the doctor's case was what struck me. He was the usual cut and dry apothecary, of no particular age and colour, with a strong Edinburgh accent and about as emotional as a bagpipe. Well, sir, he was like the rest of us; every time he looked at my prisoner, I saw that Sawbones turn sick and white with the desire to kill him.

**2**
And all the time, as we were pitching it in red hot, we were keeping the women off him as best we could for they were as wild as harpies. I never saw a circle of such hateful faces; and there was the man in the middle, with a kind of black sneering coolness – frightened too, I could see that – but carrying it off, sir, really like Satan.

**Exam-style question**

Starting with this extract, how does Stevenson present Mr Hyde as evil and menacing?

Write about:
- how Stevenson presents Mr Hyde in this extract
- how Stevenson presents Mr Hyde as evil and menacing in the novel as a whole. **(30 marks)**

Use the activities below to gather some ideas you could use in your response to the exam-style question.

1. Look at the first section from the extract above. What does this suggest about the reactions to Mr Hyde?

2. Look at the second section from the extract above. What does this suggest about Mr Hyde?

3. Think about both sections. How is Stevenson showing the reactions of Enfield, the doctor and Mr Hyde?

Think about these reactions:
- calm
- frightened
- murderous
- sweating
- sneering
- sick

4. Underline (A) short, relevant quotations in the two extracts above that you can use in your response.

5. On paper, write one or two paragraphs in response to the exam-style question above.

**Unit 2 Analysing the extract** 15

**Get back on track**

# Review your skills

### Check up

Review your response to the exam-style question on page 15. Tick ✓ the column to show how well you think you have done each of the following.

|  | Not quite ✓ | Nearly there ✓ | Got it! ✓ |
|---|---|---|---|
| made a relevant key point | ☐ | ☐ | ☐ |
| supported my key point with relevant evidence | ☐ | ☐ | ☐ |
| commented on the impact of my evidence | ☐ | ☐ | ☐ |
| responded to the question | ☐ | ☐ | ☐ |

Look over all of your work in this unit. Note down three pieces of advice on how to analyse an extract.

1. .................................................................................................
2. .................................................................................................
3. .................................................................................................

## Need more practice?

Here is another exam-style question, this time relating to the extract from Chapter 2 on page 73 (Extract A).

### Exam-style question

Starting with this extract, explore how Stevenson presents confrontations in *The Strange Case of Dr Jekyll and Mr Hyde*.

Write about:

- how Stevenson presents the confrontation in this extract
- how Stevenson presents confrontations in the novel as a whole.

(30 marks)

Write one or two paragraphs in response to this question, focusing on the extract only.

How confident do you feel about each of these **skills?** Colour in the bars.

**1** How do I choose the points I need to make?

**2** How do I develop my analysis?

**3** How do I structure a paragraph of analysis?

16  Unit 2 Analysing the extract

**Get started**

Analyse the language, form and structure used by a writer to create meanings and effects (AO2)

# ③ Commenting on the writer's choices in the extract

This unit will help you to comment on Stevenson's choices in the extract from *The Strange Case of Dr Jekyll and Mr Hyde*. The skills you will build are to:

- identify relevant language choices to comment on
- identify relevant choices of sentence form and structure to comment on
- make effective comments on the writer's choices of language, sentence form and structure.

In the exam you will face questions like the one below. This is about the extract on the next page. At the end of the unit you will **write one** or **two paragraphs** in response to this question, **focusing on the extract**.

**Exam-style question**

Starting with this extract, how does Stevenson present a sense of mystery in *The Strange Case of Dr Jekyll and Mr Hyde*?

Write about:

- how Stevenson presents a sense of mystery in this extract
- how Stevenson presents a sense of mystery in the novel as a whole.

(30 marks)

Before you tackle the question you will work through three key questions in the **skills boosts** to help you comment on the writer's choices in the extract.

① How do I identify significant language choices?
② How do I identify significant sentence forms and structural choices?
③ How do I comment on the writer's choices?

Read the extract on the next page from Chapter 8 of *The Strange Case of Dr Jekyll and Mr Hyde*.

### As you read, think about the following:

How does Stevenson present a sense of mystery *before* this extract?

How does Stevenson use characters to present a sense of mystery in this extract?

How does Stevenson use the weather and setting to present a sense of mystery in this extract?

Unit 3 Commenting on the writer's choices in the extract    17

## Get started

> **Exam-style question**
>
> Read the following extract from Chapter 8 of *The Strange Case of Dr Jekyll and Mr Hyde*.
>
> At this point in the novel, Poole comes to Mr Utterson's house as he is concerned about his master, Dr Jekyll.

**Extract A** | Chapter 8 of *The Strange Case of Dr Jekyll and Mr Hyde*

'I think there's been foul play,' said Poole, hoarsely.

'Foul play!' cried the lawyer, a good deal frightened and rather inclined to be irritated in consequence. 'What foul play! What does the man mean?'

'I daren't say, sir,' was the answer; 'but will you come along with me and see for yourself?'

5 Mr Utterson's only answer was to rise and get his hat and greatcoat; but he observed with wonder the greatness of the relief that appeared upon the butler's face, and perhaps with no less, that the wine was still untasted when he set it down to follow.

It was a wild, cold, seasonable night of March, with a pale moon, lying on her back as though the wind had tilted her, and flying wrack of the most diaphanous and lawny texture. The wind made talking difficult, and flecked the 
10 blood into the face. It seemed to have swept the streets unusually bare of passengers, besides; for Mr Utterson thought he had never seen that part of London so deserted. He could have wished it otherwise; never in his life had he been conscious of so sharp a wish to see and touch his fellow-creatures; for struggle as he might, there was borne in upon his mind a crushing anticipation of calamity. The square, when they got there, was full of wind and dust, and the thin trees in the garden were lashing themselves along the railing. Poole, who had kept all the way a 
15 pace or two ahead, now pulled up in the middle of the pavement, and in spite of the biting weather, took off his hat and mopped his brow with a red pocket-handkerchief. But for all the hurry of his coming, these were not the dews of exertion that he wiped away, but the moisture of some strangling anguish; for his face was white and his voice, when he spoke, harsh and broken.

'Well, sir,' he said, 'here we are, and God grant there be nothing wrong.'

20 'Amen, Poole,' said the lawyer.

Thereupon the servant knocked in a very guarded manner; the door was opened on the chain; and a voice asked from within, 'Is that you, Poole?'

'It's all right,' said Poole. 'Open the door.'

The hall, when they entered it, was brightly lighted up; the fire was built high; and about the hearth the whole 
25 of the servants, men and women, stood huddled together like a flock of sheep. At the sight of Mr Utterson, the housemaid broke into hysterical whimpering; and the cook, crying out 'Bless God! it's Mr Utterson,' ran forward as if to take him in her arms.

## Skills boost

### 1. How do I identify significant language choices?

Identifying significant language choices that Stevenson has made in the extract on the previous page can reveal a great deal about the characters and themes in *The Strange Case of Dr Jekyll and Mr Hyde*.

**1** Look at these sentences from the extract. They show a sense of mystery as Utterson walks through a deserted London at night.

> The wind made talking difficult, ☐   and flecked the blood into the face. ☐
>
> It seemed to have swept the streets unusually bare of passengers,
>
> besides; for Mr Utterson thought ☐   he had never seen that part of London so deserted. ☐

**a** Which sections most strongly show a sense of mystery? Tick ✓ them.

**b** Look at the sections you have ticked. Which words or phrases show a sense of mystery? Circle Ⓐ **two** choices.

**c** What does Stevenson's choice of these words and phrases suggest about the sense of mystery in these sentences? Write ✏ **one** or **two** sentences that sum up your ideas.

...........................................................................................................................................

...........................................................................................................................................

...........................................................................................................................................

**2** Look at two more sections from the extract.

**a** Annotate ✏ both sections noting what you learn from each one about a sense of mystery.

**b** Circle Ⓐ one or two words or phrases in each section that show most strongly a sense of mystery. Now annotate ✏ your choices, explaining why they convey a sense of mystery.

A
> The square, when they got there, was full of wind and dust.

B
> … these were not the dews of exertion that he wiped away, but the moisture of some strangling anguish; for his face was white and his voice, when he spoke, harsh and broken.

**3** How do the two sections above suggest a sense of mystery? Write ✏ **one** or **two sentences** explaining your idea.

...........................................................................................................................................

...........................................................................................................................................

...........................................................................................................................................

Unit 3 Commenting on the writer's choices in the extract    19

## Skills boost

### 2. How do I identify significant sentence forms and structural choices?

Writers, including Stevenson in his novel, structure their sentences to add impact to the ideas they want to convey to the reader.

Look at this section from the extract on page 18.

> Thereupon the servant knocked in a very guarded manner; the door was opened on the chain; and a voice asked from within, 'Is that you, Poole?'
> 'It's all right,' said Poole. 'Open the door.'
> The hall, when they entered it, was brightly lighted up; the fire was built high; and about the hearth the whole of the servants, men and women, stood huddled together like a flock of sheep. At the sight of Mr Utterson, the housemaid broke into hysterical whimpering; and the cook, crying out 'Bless God! it's Mr Utterson,' ran forward as if to take him in her arms.

**1** How would you describe the sense of mystery in this extract? Tick ✓ any of the sentence scraps below that accurately describe what this section suggests about a sense of mystery.

In this section of the extract, Stevenson

shows ☐    suggests ☐

a sense of mystery through the servants'

confusion ☐    annoyance ☐    relief ☐    fear ☐

**2** Look again at the extract.

**a** Identify and label ✎ **two** of the following features of sentence form in the extract above.

A. Stevenson uses a long sentence.
B. Stevenson uses a short sentence.
C. Stevenson uses a question.
D. Stevenson uses an exclamation.

**b** Now choose **one** of the sentence forms you have identified in the extract. What does your chosen sentence suggest about a sense of mystery? Write ✎ **one** sentence explaining your ideas.

In sentence ................................................, Stevenson suggests that ................................................

................................................................................................................................

**c** How does Stevenson's choice of sentence form add to the impact of this idea? Write ✎ another sentence explaining your ideas.

................................................................................................................................

................................................................................................................................

## Skills boost

# 3 How do I comment on the writer's choices?

An effective comment highlights the **choice** the writer has made, and comments on its **effect**.

Look at some of the different comments on **language** and **structure** you could make on this sentence from the extract on page 18.

> He could have wished it otherwise; never in his life had he been conscious of so sharp a wish to see and touch his fellow-creatures; for struggle as he might, there was borne in upon his mind a crushing anticipation of calamity.

### Language

You can comment on...    choice    +    effect

- the connotations or implications of a specific word or phrase

   | The phrase 'never in his life' | suggests that Utterson has not been in a situation like this before. | ☐

- a specific type of word

   | The word 'calamity' | highlights that something awful is going to happen. | ☐

- the kind of language in the whole sentence

   | The use of 'struggle', 'crushing' and 'anticipation' | helps the overall sense of mystery and potential danger. | ☐

### Structure

You can comment on...    choice    +    effect

- the length of the sentence

   | This long sentence lists the emotions Utterson is experiencing | highlighting how worried he is about Dr Jekyll and how he is expecting the worst. | ☐

- repetition

   | The repetition of 'wish' and 'wished' | emphasises how much Utterson is hoping for the best. | ☐

- the order of the words or ideas in the sentence

   | Positioning the phrase 'crushing anticipation of calamity' at the end of the sentence | gives the sense of mystery and tension greater emphasis. | ☐

(1) Which of the above would you include in your comments? Tick ✓ them.

(2) Look at another quotation from the extract on page 18.

> 'Foul play!' cried the lawyer, a good deal frightened and rather inclined to be irritated in consequence. 'What foul play! What does the man mean?'

> Think about how the use of questions creates a sense of mystery.

Write ✏ **one** or **two** sentences on paper commenting on Stevenson's choices of language and structure in this quotation.

**Unit 3 Commenting on the writer's choices in the extract** 21

# Commenting on the writer's choices in the extract

**Get back on track**

To comment effectively on Stevenson's choices in the extract, you need to:
- identify relevant evidence from the extract to support your ideas
- select significant choices of language and/or sentence form and/or structure in the evidence you have identified
- highlight the choices that Stevenson has made in your evidence and comment on their effect.

(For more help on structuring a paragraph of analysis, see Unit 2.)

Look at the exam-style question you saw at the start of the unit on page 17.

**Exam-style question**

Starting with this extract, how does Stevenson present a sense of mystery in *The Strange Case of Dr Jekyll and Mr Hyde*?

1. Can you identify all the different things the student has included in this paragraph?
Link ✏️ the annotations to the paragraph to show where the student has included them.

**Key features of an effective paragraph of analysis:**

- key point focusing on the key words in the question
- evidence from the text to support the point
- comments on the evidence and its impact
- a response to the question

Stevenson presents a sense of mystery when Poole comes to Utterson's house. The repetition of the short exclamation 'foul play' invites the reader to be concerned about what is about to be revealed. Utterson then walks with Poole to Jekyll's laboratory, and the weather and atmosphere help to intensify the sense of mystery as 'lashing' winds have caused the streets to be abandoned and eerily quiet. By using long sentences, which slow the pace and build a sense of dread, to describe Utterson's inner thoughts, the mystery is built up and we are expecting the worst when Poole and Utterson arrive at the house. By the time they get there, Utterson has a 'crushing anticipation of calamity' and Poole is experiencing 'strangling anguish'. By using the verbs 'crushing' and 'strangling', Stevenson builds the mystery as we can feel the tension impacting on the characters. The mysteriousness of the situation is then further underlined by the use of religious language such as 'Amen' and the exclamation – 'Bless God!' as everyone prays for the best, but still there has been no explanation for the anxiety shown by the characters.

**Key features of an effective comment on the writer's choices:**

- comments on Stevenson's language choice(s)
- comments on Stevenson's choice(s) of structure or sentence form

22 Unit 3 Commenting on the writer's choices in the extract

**Get back on track**

# Your turn!

You are now going to **write one** or **two paragraphs** in response to the exam-style question below, focusing on Extract A on page 18.

> **Exam-style question**
>
> Starting with this extract, how does Stevenson present a sense of mystery in *The Strange Case of Dr Jekyll and Mr Hyde*?
>
> Write about:
> - how Stevenson presents a sense of mystery in this extract
> - how Stevenson presents a sense of mystery in the novel as a whole.
>
> (30 marks)

1. Choose **one short section** from the extract on page 18 that clearly suggests a sense of mystery. Highlight it.

2. Now look closely at the section you have chosen. Select **one** short quotation that clearly shows how a sense of mystery is presented. Underline it.

3. Think about words or phrases in your chosen section that make a significant contribution to your answer. What do these say about your impressions of a sense of mystery?

   a. Which words or phrases reveal something significant about the sense of mystery at this point in the novel? Circle them.

   b. How do these words and phrases show the characters' thoughts and feelings about the sense of mystery? Add to your annotations.

4. Now think about Stevenson's choices of structure or sentence form in your chosen quotation. Think about:
   - the length of the sentence(s)
   - the order of the words or ideas in the sentence(s)
   - any repetition.

   Do Stevenson's choices of structure or sentence form in your chosen section make a significant contribution to your impression of a sense of mystery? How? Annotate your chosen section with your ideas.

5. Using all the ideas you have noted, write **one** paragraph in response to the exam-style question above.

   ........................................................................................................................
   ........................................................................................................................
   ........................................................................................................................
   ........................................................................................................................

6. Repeat questions 1–5, focusing on a different section of the extract.

**Unit 3 Commenting on the writer's choices in the extract**

# Review your skills

**Get back on track**

## Check up

Review your response to the exam-style question on page 23. Tick ✓ the column to show how well you think you have done each of the following.

|  | Not quite ✓ | Nearly there ✓ | Got it! ✓ |
|---|---|---|---|
| structured an effective paragraph of analysis in response to the question | ☐ | ☐ | ☐ |
| commented on Stevenson's language choices | ☐ | ☐ | ☐ |
| commented on Stevenson's choices of structure and/or sentence form | ☐ | ☐ | ☐ |

## Need more practice?

Here is another exam-style question, this time relating to the extract from Chapter 9 on page 74 (Extract B).

### Exam-style question

Starting with this extract, how does Stevenson present science and the supernatural in *The Strange Case of Dr Jekyll and Mr Hyde*?

Write about:
- how Stevenson presents science and the supernatural in this extract
- how Stevenson presents science and the supernatural in the novel as a whole.

(30 marks)

Write ✎ **one** or **two** paragraphs on paper in response to this question, focusing on language and structure **in the extract only**.

How confident do you feel about each of these **skills?** Colour ✎ in the bars.

1. How do I identify significant language choices?
2. How do I identify significant sentence forms and structural choices?
3. How do I comment on the writer's choices?

24     Unit 3 Commenting on the writer's choices in the extract

**Get started**   Read, understand and respond to texts (AO1)

#  Exploring themes and characters

This unit will help you to explore how the characters and themes of *The Strange Case of Dr Jekyll and Mr Hyde* develop in the novel and help you to develop your response to them. The skills you will build are to:

- track how characters develop in the novel
- explore themes in the novel
- comment on the development of characters and themes in the novel.

In the exam you will face questions like the one below. This is about the extract on the next page. At the end of the unit you will **plan** and **write one** or **two paragraphs** in response to this question.

> **Exam-style question**
>
> Starting with this extract, how does Stevenson present the theme of the duality of human nature in *The Strange Case of Dr Jekyll and Mr Hyde*?
>
> Write about:
> - how how Stevenson presents the duality of human nature in this extract
> - how Stevenson presents the duality of human nature in the novel as a whole.
>
> (30 marks)

Before you tackle the question you will work through three key questions in the **skills boosts** to help you explore the novel's themes and characters.

 How do I track the development of a character?

 How do I explore a theme?

 How do I comment on the development of character or theme?

Read the extract on the next page from Chapter 10 of *The Strange Case of Dr Jekyll and Mr Hyde*.

Think about the idea that every human is capable of good and evil.

## As you read, think about the following:

| What has happened before this extract? What happens after this extract? | How does Stevenson present the theme of the duality of human nature in the extract? | What impact does the scene described have on the reader? |

Unit 4 Exploring themes and characters  25

# Get started

> **Exam-style question**
>
> Read the following extract from Chapter 10 of *The Strange Case of Dr Jekyll and Mr Hyde*.
>
> At this point in the novel, Dr Jekyll talks about his early life and his struggle with the two sides of his personality.

**Extract A | Chapter 10 of *The Strange Case of Dr Jekyll and Mr Hyde***

I was born in the year 18—to a large fortune, endowed besides with excellent parts, inclined by nature to industry, fond of the respect of the wise and good among my fellowmen, and thus, as might have been supposed, with every guarantee of an honourable and distinguished future. And indeed the worst of my faults was a certain impatient gaiety of disposition, such as has made the happiness of many, but such as I found it hard to reconcile with my
5  imperious desire to carry my head high, and wear a more than commonly grave countenance before the public. Hence it came about that I concealed my pleasures; and that when I reached years of reflection, and began to look round me and take stock of my progress and position in the world, I stood already committed to a profound duplicity of life. Many a man would have even blazoned such irregularities as I was guilty of; but from the high views that I had set before me, I regarded and hid them with an almost morbid sense of shame. It was thus rather the
10  exacting nature of my aspirations than any particular degradation in my faults, that made me what I was, and, with even a deeper trench than in the majority of men, severed in me those provinces of good and ill which divide and compound man's dual nature. In this case, I was driven to reflect deeply and inveterately on that hard law of life, which lies at the root of religion and is one of the most plentiful springs of distress. Though so profound a double-dealer, I was in no sense a hypocrite; both sides of me were in dead earnest; I was no more myself when I laid aside
15  restraint and plunged in shame, than when I laboured, in the eye of day, at the furtherance of knowledge or the relief of sorrow and suffering. And it chanced that the direction of my scientific studies, which led wholly towards the mystic and the transcendental, reacted and shed a strong light on this consciousness of the perennial war among my members. With every day, and from both sides of my intelligence, the moral and the intellectual, I thus drew steadily nearer to that truth, by whose partial discovery I have been doomed to such a dreadful shipwreck:
20  that man is not truly one, but truly two.

## Skills boost

### 1  How do I track the development of a character?

Dr Jekyll is the key character in *The Strange Case of Dr Jekyll and Mr Hyde*. To write effectively about him in the novel as a whole, you need to think about Stevenson's presentation of **how** he develops and **why**.

**1** Think about how Dr Jekyll is presented in the **first three chapters** of the novel.

| He is a doctor with a good reputation and is well regarded by others. | He refuses to talk about his relationship with Mr Hyde. | He has some alternative ideas about science. |

How would you sum up the character of Dr Jekyll at the start of the novel? Tick ☐ any of the words below and/or add ✎ your own ideas.

| mysterious | professional | friendly | quiet | respectable | unconventional | secretive | |
| ☐ | ☐ | ☐ | ☐ | ☐ | ☐ | ☐ | ☐ |

**2** Now think about how Dr Jekyll is presented in the **last two chapters** of the novel.

| He is fighting against his alter ego Mr Hyde and contacts Dr Lanyon for help. |
| He is taken over by Hyde and takes his own life. |

How would you sum up the character of Dr Jekyll at the end of the novel? Write ✎ up to five words.

> Look at the words you chose to describe him in question 1. What has changed?

| | | | | |
|---|---|---|---|---|

**3** Look at some of the key events in the novel showing the development of Dr Jekyll's character.

**Ch. 5**  Hyde's involvement in the murder of Danvers Carew is revealed.
Jekyll greets Utterson with a 'changed voice'.
He worries about his reputation.    /10

**Ch. 6**  Dr Lanyon becomes ill.
Jekyll renews his social life.
He is happy and normal.    /10

**Ch. 7 and 8**  Jekyll is seen at a window and Utterson breaks into his laboratory.
There are signs Hyde has taken over Jekyll.
Jekyll's new will is found with a note to Utterson.    /10

How significant are these scenes in showing the change in Dr Jekyll's character in the novel? Give ✎ each one a mark out of ten: 1/10 = not at all significant; 10/10 = highly significant.

**Unit 4 Exploring themes and characters**    27

## Skills boost

### 2. How do I explore a theme?

To explore how Stevenson presents a theme in the novel, you need to identify key events in which that theme is featured.

**1)** Look at some of the **key themes** in *The Strange Case of Dr Jekyll and Mr Hyde* below. Complete these notes with a **key event** in which each theme is relevant.

| duality of human nature | |
| --- | --- |
| good and evil | the evil Mr Hyde tramples over the innocent girl |
| science | |
| secrets and reputation | |
| appearance and reality | |
| violence and horror | The maid witnesses Sir Danvers Carew being beaten to death. |

**2)** A **key theme** is an idea that Stevenson explores in different ways at different points in the novel. Look at some of the key points in the novel in which Stevenson explores the theme of **science**.

| Dr Lanyon has a practical and conventional view of science. | Dr Jekyll is more experimental in his approach. | Dr Jekyll's experiments to become Mr Hyde become more dangerous as the novel progresses. | These experiments ultimately kill Dr Lanyon and Dr Jekyll. |

How does Stevenson present science in the novel? Tick ✓ any of the ideas below.

| ✓ Positive | ✓ Neutral | ✓ Negative |
| --- | --- | --- |
| Doctors are respected in society | It explains how Mr Hyde is created | dangerous |
| It has a practical and mystical power | | deadly |

**3)** Now think about **the theme of the duality of human nature** in the novel.

**a** Note down **two** or **three** significant key events in the novel that feature the duality of human nature.

..................................................................................................

..................................................................................................

**b** How does Stevenson present the theme of duality of human nature in the novel? Write **one** or **two** sentences explaining your ideas.

..................................................................................................

28  Unit 4 Exploring themes and characters

## Skills boost

### 3 How do I comment on the development of character or theme?

One way to explore how characters and themes develop in a novel is to **compare** how they are presented at different key points in the novel.

Look at the key points below, which show Dr Jekyll's changing state of mind in the story.

A. I am painfully situated, Utterson; my position is … a very strange one.

B. I stood already committed to a profound duplicity of life.

C. I knew myself, at the first breath of this new life, to be more wicked, tenfold more wicked, sold a slave to my original evil; and the thought, in that moment, braced and delighted me like wine.

D. If I am the chief of sinners, I am the chief of sufferers also.

E. … that man is not truly one, but truly two.

F. For two months … I led a life of such severity as I had never before attained to.

G. … before the smile was struck out of his face and succeeded by an expression of such abject terror and despair …

1. 
   a. Which of these key points show that Dr Jekyll is struggling with his state of mind? Circle Ⓐ them.
   b. Which of these key points show that Dr Jekyll is accepting his situation? Underline Ⓐ them.
   c. What effect does Dr Jekyll's changing state of mind have on the reader? Write ✎ **one** or **two** sentences explaining your ideas.

   ................................................................................................
   ................................................................................................

2. Look at these four key moments in the novel in which the theme of **horror** is shown.

   Ch. 1 | Enfield recounts the tale of Hyde trampling the young girl.

   Ch. 2 | Utterson describes Hyde as a monstrous figure.

   Ch. 4 | The maid witnesses the murder of Carew.

   Ch. 9 | Lanyon's letter outlines Hyde's transformation into Dr Jekyll

   a. Think about how the theme of horror is presented in the novel. Tick ✓ any of the statements below that you agree with.

   | Horror highlights the danger of science. | ☐ | The horror is heightened by the descriptions of the settings. | ☐ |
   | Horror is used to build tension. | ☐ | The horrific scenes help explain the duality of human nature. | ☐ |

   b. Write ✎ on paper **one** or **two** sentences summing up your thoughts about how the presentation of horror in *The Strange Case of Dr Jekyll and Mr Hyde* is used to shock the reader.

**Get back on track**

# Exploring themes and characters

To explore the themes and characters in *The Strange Case of Dr Jekyll and Mr Hyde* effectively, you need to:
- identify significant key events in the novel in which those characters or themes are shown
- compare how they are presented in those key events.

Look at this exam-style question you saw at the start of the unit.

**Exam-style question**

Starting with this extract, how does Stevenson present the theme of the duality of human nature in *The Strange Case of Dr Jekyll and Mr Hyde*?

Write about:
- how Stevenson presents the duality of human nature in this extract
- how Stevenson presents the duality of human nature in the novel as a whole.

1. Now look at these two paragraphs, written by a student in response to the exam-style question above.

> Throughout the novel, Stevenson presents the idea of the duality of human nature through the actions and thoughts of Dr Jekyll. In Chapter 6, we begin to see how Dr Jekyll's mood and actions have changed. At the beginning of the chapter, we are told that he is 'at peace' and has been going out in public and seeing friends. But by the end of the chapter he is refusing to see Utterson and sends him a mysterious note stating that 'If I am the chief of sinners, I am the chief of sufferers also'. Stevenson presents Dr Jekyll here as a man who is tormented by the duality of human nature and is suffering for all of the sins he has committed.
>
> This impression of the duality of human nature is heightened in Chapter 9. Dr Lanyon receives a mysterious letter from Dr Jekyll and is asked to invite a monstrous-looking man into his house. The man takes a potion and transforms into Dr Jekyll. Lanyon sees first-hand what we as readers have long suspected – that Dr Jekyll and Mr Hyde are the same person – and reveals how good and evil can exist in that same person. This lasting and powerful image from Lanyon is told in the first person so we can realise the true horror and shock of the situation with him.

   a. Circle (A) and label (✏) **all** the key events in the novel that this student has referred to in these paragraphs.

   b. Underline (A) and label (✏) where in these paragraphs this student **comments** on how Stevenson presents the duality of human nature in these key events.

   c. Highlight (✏) and label (✏) where in these paragraphs this student **compares** key events in which the duality of human nature is presented in the novel as a whole to develop their ideas.

Unit 4 Exploring themes and characters

# Your turn!

You are now going to **write two paragraphs** in response to the exam-style question.

> **Exam-style question**
>
> Starting with this extract, how does Stevenson present the theme of the duality of human nature in *The Strange Case of Dr Jekyll and Mr Hyde*?
>
> Write about:
> - how Stevenson presents the duality of human nature in this extract
> - how Stevenson presents the duality of human nature in the novel as a whole.
>
> (30 marks)

**1** Which key scenes or events in the novel could you focus on in your response? Note **four** of your ideas below.

Think about:

> ? What does each of these events suggest about the theme of the duality of human nature?

> ? Is the theme of the duality of human nature always presented in this way? Or are there other key events in the novel which present this theme in a different light?

1

2

3

4

**2** Now compare how the theme of the duality of human nature is presented in the different key events you have noted above. What does your comparison suggest about the way in which the duality of human nature is presented in the novel? Add to your notes.

**3** Use your notes above to write **two** paragraphs on paper in response to the exam-style question.

**Unit 4 Exploring themes and characters**

# Review your skills

## Check up

Review your response to the exam-style question on page 31. Tick ✓ the column to show how well you think you have done each of the following.

|  | Not quite ✓ | Nearly there ✓ | Got it! ✓ |
|---|---|---|---|
| identified significant key events in the novel showing the theme of the duality of human nature | ☐ | ☐ | ☐ |
| commented on how the duality of human nature is presented in each significant key event | ☐ | ☐ | ☐ |
| developed my ideas by comparing how the duality of human nature is presented in key events | ☐ | ☐ | ☐ |

## Need more practice?

Here is another exam-style question, this time relating to the extract from Chapter 9 on page 74 (Extract B).

### Exam-style question

Starting with this extract, how does Stevenson present horrific events in *The Strange Case of Dr Jekyll and Mr Hyde*?

Write about:
- how Stevenson presents horrific events in this extract
- how Stevenson presents horrific events in the novel as a whole.

(30 marks)

Write ✏ **two** paragraphs in response to this question, focusing on the second bullet point: **the novel as a whole.**

How confident do you feel about each of these **skills?** Colour ✏ in the bars.

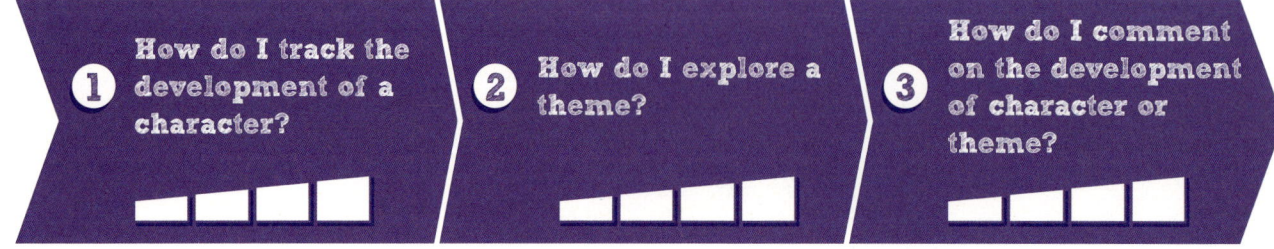

1. How do I track the development of a character?
2. How do I explore a theme?
3. How do I comment on the development of character or theme?

32  Unit 4 Exploring themes and characters

**Get started**    Read, understand and respond to texts (AO1)

# ⑤ Planning your response

This unit will help you to plan your response to the exam question. The skills you will build are to:

- develop a critical judgement in response to the focus of the exam question
- support your judgement with relevant points
- sequence your points to build a successful argument in support of your judgement.

In the exam you will face a question like the one below. This is about the extract on the next page. At the end of the unit you will **write your own response** to this question.

> **Exam-style question**
>
> Starting with this extract, how does Stevenson present the theme of secrecy in *The Strange Case of Dr Jekyll and Mr Hyde*?
>
> Write about:
> - how Stevenson presents the theme of secrecy in this extract
> - how Stevenson presents the theme of secrecy in the novel as a whole.
>
> (30 marks)

Before you tackle the question you will work through three key questions in the **skills boosts** to help you plan your response.

① How do I make a critical judgement?    ② How do I gather relevant points?    ③ How do I sequence my points?

Read the extract on the next page from Chapter 6 of *The Strange Case of Dr Jekyll and Mr Hyde*.

### As you read, think about the following: ✓

- What has happened before this extract? What happens after this extract?
- How does Stevenson present the theme of secrecy in this extract?
- How does this compare with how the theme of secrecy is presented in the novel?

Unit 5 Planning your response    33

### Get started

> **Exam-style question**
>
> Read the following extract from Chapter 6 of *The Strange Case of Dr Jekyll and Mr Hyde*.
>
> At this point in the novel, Utterson tries to resolve the conflict between Lanyon and Jekyll.

**Extract A** | Chapter 6 of *The Strange Case of Dr Jekyll and Mr Hyde*

'Jekyll is ill, too,' observed Utterson. 'Have you seen him?'
But Lanyon's face changed, and he held up a trembling hand. 'I wish to see or hear no more of Dr Jekyll,' he said in a loud, unsteady voice. 'I am quite done with that person; and I beg that you will spare me any allusion to one whom I regard as dead.'

5  'Tut-tut,' said Mr Utterson; and then after a considerable pause, 'Can't I do anything?' he inquired. 'We are three very old friends, Lanyon; we shall not live to make others.'
'Nothing can be done,' returned Lanyon; 'ask himself.'
'He will not see me,' said the lawyer.
'I am not surprised at that,' was the reply. 'Some day, Utterson, after I am dead, you may perhaps come to learn the
10  right and wrong of this. I cannot tell you. And in the meantime, if you can sit and talk with me of other things, for God's sake, stay and do so; but if you cannot keep clear of this accursed topic, then in God's name, go, for I cannot bear it.'
As soon as he got home, Utterson sat down and wrote to Jekyll, complaining of his exclusion from the house, and asking the cause of this unhappy break with Lanyon; and the next day brought him a long answer, often very
15  pathetically worded, and sometimes darkly mysterious in drift. The quarrel with Lanyon was incurable. 'I do not blame our old friend,' Jekyll wrote, 'but I share his view that we must never meet. I mean from henceforth to lead a life of extreme seclusion; you must not be surprised, nor must you doubt my friendship, if my door is often shut even to you. You must suffer me to go my own dark way. I have brought on myself a punishment and a danger that I cannot name. If I am the chief of sinners, I am the chief of sufferers also. I could not think that this earth contained
20  a place for sufferings and terrors so unmanning; and you can do but one thing, Utterson, to lighten this destiny, and that is to respect my silence.' Utterson was amazed; the dark influence of Hyde had been withdrawn, the doctor had returned to his old tasks and amities; a week ago, the prospect had smiled with every promise of a cheerful and an honoured age; and now in a moment, friendship, and peace of mind, and the whole tenor of his life were wrecked. So great and unprepared a change pointed to madness; but in view of Lanyon's manner and words, there
25  must lie for it some deeper ground.

## Skills boost

# 1  How do I make a critical judgement?

Before you plan your written response, you need to make a **critical judgement**. This means weighing up the key evidence in the novel and coming to a conclusion: a sentence or two that sum up your ideas.

**(1)** One way to begin developing your critical judgement is to focus on the extract you are given in the question. Look at the exam-style question and two sections below from the extract on page 34.

> **Exam-style question**
>
> Starting with this extract, how does Stevenson present (the theme of secrecy)?

> 'Some day, Utterson, after I am dead, you may perhaps come to learn the right and wrong of this. I cannot tell you. And in the meantime, if you can sit and talk with me of other things, for God's sake, stay and do so; but if you cannot keep clear of this accursed topic, then in God's name, go, for I cannot bear it.'

*Refuses to speak about the incident; will never tell while he is alive.*

> 'I do not blame our old friend,' Jekyll wrote, 'but I share his view that we must never meet. I mean from henceforth to lead a life of extreme seclusion; you must not be surprised, nor must you doubt my friendship, if my door is often shut even to you.'

**a** Explore each aspect of the question's focus – in this case, the theme of secrecy. Annotate the short extracts above with your thoughts about the importance of keeping secrets.

**b** Write one or two sentences summing up your **critical judgement** on how secrets and secrecy are presented in these extracts.

...........................................................................................................................................................

...........................................................................................................................................................

**(2)** Now you need to think about how the theme of secrecy is explored in the **novel as a whole**. Look at these other key events in the novel in which secrets are shown.

| Ch. 1 | Utterson tries to protect Jekyll's reputation. | Ch. 5 | Utterson suspects Jekyll forged Hyde's letter. | Ch. 10 | Jekyll's confession and statement. |

**a** Which of these key events could be used as evidence to **support** or **develop** the critical judgement that you made in **(1) b**? Tick ✓ them.

**b** Now that you have considered other key events from the novel as a whole, rewrite your critical judgement on how Stevenson presents the theme of secrecy in *The Strange Case of Dr Jekyll and Mr Hyde*.

...........................................................................................................................................................

...........................................................................................................................................................

...........................................................................................................................................................

**Unit 5 Planning your response**

## Skills boost

### 2 How do I gather relevant points?

You need to gather a range of points from the extract and from the whole novel to support and develop the critical judgement you make in response to the exam question.

**(1)** Think about how the theme of secrecy is presented **in the extract** on page 34 and **in the whole novel**.

**a** Look at some different critical judgements about the presentation of the theme of secrecy in *The Strange Case of Dr Jekyll and Mr Hyde* below. For each one, circle (A) the number on the scale to show how strongly you agree or disagree.

|   | | Disagree | Unsure | Agree |
|---|---|---|---|---|
| A | Secrets are essential to Dr Jekyll's experiments. | 1 | 2 | 3 |
| B | The way secrets are kept and revealed ensures the reader is engaged and intrigued. | 1 | 2 | 3 |
| C | Secrets are mainly used to protect the characters' reputations. | 1 | 2 | 3 |
| D | The reader sympathises with characters who keep secrets. | 1 | 2 | 3 |
| E | Keeping secrets is dangerous and has consequences for other characters. | 1 | 2 | 3 |

**b** Now look at some of the key events from the novel below. Select key events that support each of the judgements that you agreed with, labelling ✏ them **A, B, C**, etc. to show which judgement they support.

**Chapter 1**
- a Enfield believes that a respectable man is paying Hyde to keep a secret from his past from being revealed.
- b Enfield and Utterson agree to keep quiet.

**Chapter 2**
- a Utterson vows to 'seek' Mr 'Hyde' and find out his secret past.
- b Mr Hyde disappears into the doorway and refuses to speak.

**Chapter 5**
- a Jekyll asks Utterson to keep a letter written by Hyde.
- b Utterson suspects Jekyll forged the letter but locks it in a safe.

**Chapter 8**
- a Poole reveals the requests for chemicals from Dr Jekyll, who is hidden away.
- b After Hyde's death, Utterson leaves and takes the two secret letters with him.

**(2) a** Review all of your answers on this page so far. Use them to note ✏ down in the table **three** key points you might make in your response to the exam-style question.

**b** For each key point, note ✏ the key scenes from the novel that you could refer to as **evidence** to support your point.

| | Key point | Evidence |
|---|---|---|
| 1 | | |
| 2 | | |
| 3 | | |

36    **Unit 5 Planning your response**

## Skills boost

### 3 How do I sequence my points?

You need to sequence your key points to build a response that supports your critical judgement. You need to start with the extract – but where do you go from there?

Look at this exam-style question, and one student's critical judgement in response to it.

**Exam-style question**

Starting with this extract, how does Stevenson present the theme of secrets?

> Stevenson presents secrecy as a point of conflict and concern for all of the characters. Lanyon suggests to Utterson that he might learn the truth once he has died – he will never tell Utterson.

Now look at these four key points, taken from the same student's plan:

A | Jekyll refuses to discuss Hyde with Utterson

B | Secret letter from Lanyon to Utterson

C | Utterson locks up Hyde's confession letter

D | Poole runs secret errands for Jekyll

**1** One way to sequence the key points in a response is to work your way through the novel **chronologically**: exploring how a character or theme develops as the story progresses.

How would you sequence the four key points above if you were organising this response **chronologically**? Write ✏ the letters **A–D** in the order in which you would sequence them.

☐ ☐ ☐ ☐

**2** Another way to organise the key points in a response is to **synthesise** your key points: grouping related points together.

For example, you could:

> **chronological:** in time order
> **synthesise:** combine or group together

**a** group your key points by **character**. ☐

How would you sequence the key points above if you were going to explore how Stevenson presents the secrets of one **character** and then another? Write ✏ the letters A–D.

☐ ☐ ☐ ☐

Or you could:

**b** group your key points by **approach**. ☐

How would you sequence the key points above if you were going to look at one way in which Stevenson presents secrecy, and then another way in which he does this? ✏

☐ ☐ ☐ ☐

**3** Look at all of your answers above.

**a** Which method would **you** choose to sequence the key points above? Tick ✓ it.

**b** Write ✏ **one** or **two** sentences explaining your choice.

......................................................................................

......................................................................................

Unit 5 Planning your response    37

# Planning your response

> To plan an effective response, you need to:
> - make a critical judgement summing up your response to the focus of the question
> - gather relevant points: identify the key moments in the novel that support your critical judgement and use them to develop points you can make in your response
> - sequence your points: decide on the most effective way to build a response that supports your critical judgement: for example, chronologically, or by character, or by approach.

Look at this exam-style question you saw at the start of the unit.

**Exam-style question**

Starting with this extract, how does Stevenson present the theme of secrecy in *The Strange Case of Dr Jekyll and Mr Hyde*?

Write about:
- how Stevenson presents the theme of secrecy in this extract
- how Stevenson presents the theme of secrecy in the novel as a whole.

(1) Now look at these two paragraphs, written by a student in response to the exam-style question above.

> In 'The Strange Case of Dr Jekyll and Mr Hyde', Stevenson presents the theme of secrecy within the novel as something which is dangerous and could bring down a man's reputation and life. We are introduced to the idea of secrets in Chapter 1, when both Utterson and Enfield agree to never speak of the incident with Mr Hyde again as they believe he is blackmailing someone they know. Stevenson uses this secret to show how secrets are powerful, and that people would pay to keep their secrets safe.
>
> Likewise, Dr Jekyll protects his own secret and reputation – that he has an alter ego called Mr Hyde. In chapter 3, Stevenson creates the secretive mysterious doctor who refuses to talk about his relationship with Mr Hyde to anyone and slowly begins to shut himself away from his friends to work on his experiments and become Mr Hyde. This use of secrecy as a way to build tension and mystery is heightened when Lanyon keeps the results of these experiments secret because he is so horrified by the truth and does not want others to know about it. Stevenson ensures that we as readers do not find out the truth until Lanyon's letter is read in chapter 9, which builds the suspense as we do not know why Lanyon is so desperate to keep the secret until that point.

Write ✏ **one** sentence summarising the critical judgement that these paragraphs support.

...........................................................................................................................

...........................................................................................................................

(2) Circle Ⓐ all the key events in the novel that these paragraphs use to support the critical response.

(3) How has this student organised their key points? Tick ✓ one.

- A  chronologically  ☐
- B  by character     ☐
- C  by approach      ☐

38    Unit 5 Planning your response

# Your turn!

You are now going to **write your own answer** in response to the exam-style question.

> **Exam-style question**
>
> Starting with this extract, how does Stevenson explore the theme of secrecy in *The Strange Case of Dr Jekyll and Mr Hyde*?
>
> Write about:
> - how Stevenson presents the theme of secrecy in this extract
> - how Stevenson presents the theme of secrecy in the novel as a whole.
>
> (30 marks)

1. Sum up your **critical judgement** in response to the exam-style question above. This will be the **conclusion** that your response must support.

   ....................................................................................................................................................
   ....................................................................................................................................................
   ....................................................................................................................................................

2. Which **key events** in the novel will you explore in your response to support your critical judgement? Note them below.

   [ ]

3. Note down all the **key points** you will make about these key events or scenes to support your critical judgement.

   ....................................................................................................................................................
   ....................................................................................................................................................
   ....................................................................................................................................................
   ....................................................................................................................................................

4. **a** How will you sequence your key points? Tick ✓ **one** answer.

   chronologically [ ]     by character [ ]     by approach [ ]

   **b** Number your key points in ③, sequencing them to build a response that supports your critical judgement.

5. Now write your response to the exam-style question above on paper.

**Unit 5 Planning your response**

**Get back on track**

# Review your skills

## Check up

Review your response to the exam-style question on page 39. Tick ✓ the column to show how well you think you have done each of the following.

|  | Not quite ✓ | Nearly there ✓ | Got it! ✓ |
|---|---|---|---|
| made a critical judgement | ☐ | ☐ | ☐ |
| made key points using key scenes and events in the novel to support my critical judgement | ☐ | ☐ | ☐ |
| sequenced my key points to build a response that supports my critical judgement | ☐ | ☐ | ☐ |

Look over all of your work in this unit. Note down the **three** most important things to remember when planning your response.

1. ...................................................................................................................
2. ...................................................................................................................
3. ...................................................................................................................

## Need more practice?

Here is another exam-style question, this time relating to the extract from Chapter 1 on page 75 (Extract C).

### Exam-style question

Starting with this extract, how does Stevenson present Victorian respectability in *The Strange Case of Dr Jekyll and Mr Hyde*?

Write about:
- how Stevenson presents Victorian respectability in this extract
- how Stevenson presents Victorian respectability in the novel as a whole.

(30 marks)

Plan your response to this question. Aim to:
- sum up your critical judgement in one or two sentences
- identify key events to focus on, and key points to make
- sequence your ideas.

How confident do you feel about each of these **skills**? Colour in the bars.

**① How do I make a critical judgement?**

**② How do I gather relevant points?**

**③ How do I sequence my points?**

40    Unit 5 Planning your response

**Get started**

Read, understand and respond to texts (AO1); Analyse the language, form and structure used by a writer to create meanings and effects (AO2)

# 6 Writing your response

This unit will help you write the part of your response in which you have to focus on **the novel as a whole**. The skills you will build are to:

- know key events and key quotations you can use when writing about the novel as a whole
- understand how to use key events and quotations as evidence
- be able to analyse evidence from the novel effectively.

In the exam you will face a question like the one below. This is about the extract on the next page. At the end of the unit you will **plan your own response** to this question.

**Reminder:** For more help on writing about **the extract**, see Units 2 and 3.

**Exam-style question**

Starting with this extract, how does Stevenson present tension in *The Strange Case of Dr Jekyll and Mr Hyde?*

Write about:

- how how Stevenson presents tension in this extract
- how how Stevenson presents tension in the novel as a whole.

(30 marks)

Before you tackle the question you will work through three key questions in the **skills boosts** to help you write your response.

1. How do I choose key events and key quotations to learn?
2. How do I use evidence to support my ideas?
3. How do I analyse my evidence?

Read the extract on the next page from Chapter 4 of *The Strange Case of Dr Jekyll and Mr Hyde*.

**As you read, think about the following:**

What has happened before this extract? What happens after this extract?

How does Stevenson use setting and atmosphere in this extract?

How does Stevenson present tension in this extract?

**Unit 6 Writing your response** 41

### Get started

> **Exam-style question**
>
> Read the following extract from Chapter 4 of *The Strange Case of Dr Jekyll and Mr Hyde*.
>
> At this point in the novel, a maid witnesses a horrific event from her window.

**Extract A** | Chapter 4 of *The Strange Case of Dr Jekyll and Mr Hyde*

A maid servant living alone in a house not far from the river, had gone upstairs to bed about eleven. Although a fog rolled over the city in the small hours, the early part of the night was cloudless, and the lane, which the maid's window overlooked, was brilliantly lit by the full moon. It seems she was romantically given, for she sat down upon her box, which stood immediately under the window, and fell into a dream of musing. Never (she used to
5   say, with streaming tears, when she narrated that experience), never had she felt more at peace with all men or thought more kindly of the world. And as she so sat she became aware of an aged beautiful gentleman with white hair, drawing near along the lane; and advancing to meet him, another and very small gentleman, to whom at first she paid less attention. When they had come within speech (which was just under the maid's eyes) the older man bowed and accosted the other with a very pretty manner of politeness. It did not seem as if the subject of his
10  address were of great importance; indeed, from his pointing, it some times appeared as if he were only inquiring his way; but the moon shone on his face as he spoke, and the girl was pleased to watch it, it seemed to breathe such an innocent and old-world kindness of disposition, yet with something high too, as of a well-founded self-content. Presently her eye wandered to the other, and she was surprised to recognise in him a certain Mr Hyde, who had once visited her master and for whom she had conceived a dislike. He had in his hand a heavy cane, with
15  which he was trifling; but he answered never a word, and seemed to listen with an ill-contained impatience. And then all of a sudden he broke out in a great flame of anger, stamping with his foot, brandishing the cane, and carrying on (as the maid described it) like a madman. The old gentleman took a step back, with the air of one very much surprised and a trifle hurt; and at that Mr Hyde broke out of all bounds and clubbed him to the earth. And next moment, with ape-like fury, he was trampling his victim under foot and hailing down a storm of blows, under
20  which the bones were audibly shattered and the body jumped upon the roadway. At the horror of these sights and sounds, the maid fainted.

## Skills boost

### 1 How do I choose key events and key quotations to learn?

When you write about the **extract**, you should support your response with quotations from the extract. When you write about the **novel as a whole**, you should refer to key events. You can also use some key quotations that you have learned to show your detailed understanding of the novel.

**Reminder:** For more help on writing about the extract, see Units 2 and 3.

The key events in the novel are those that show a significant aspect of, or development in, a key character **or** explore a key theme.

(1) Look at the extract on page 42. Which of the key characters and themes below are significant in this part of Chapter 4? Circle (A) them.

| Characters |
|---|
| Hyde |
| Jekyll |
| Utterson |
| Danvers Carew |
| Poole |

| Themes |
|---|
| Horror |
| Appearances and reality |
| Violence |
| Good and Evil |
| Science |
| Atmosphere |
| Victorian London |

Think about what is being described and how it is being described.

(2) Now look at some of the other events in Chapter 4.

A | The body is found with Utterson's name and address on it.

B | Utterson recognises the broken cane used to beat Carew as belonging to Mr Hyde

C | Utterson travels through the eerie London streets and observes people and buildings

D | Hyde is not at home; his rooms are in a mess and the rest of the cane is in the room

**a** Which events reveal something about a key character? Label 🖉 them with that character's name.

**b** Which events explore a key theme? Label 🖉 them with the name of the key theme.

**c** Which key events in Chapter 4 should you make sure you know? Tick ✓ them.

(3) A | A great chocolate-coloured pall lowered over heaven (Chapter 4)

B | I thought, a change – he seemed to swell – his face became suddenly black (Chapter 9)

C | That masked thing, like a monkey (Chapter 8)

D | man is not truly one, but truly two (Chapter 10)

**a** Which quotation (A, B, C or D) most effectively shows tension **and** reveals something about a key character in the novel? Tick ✓ one.

The best quotations to learn are short, and can be used to support two (or more) different ideas.

**b** Look at the quotation you have chosen. How could you make it shorter and easier to learn by heart? Underline (A) the most significant or revealing phrase of five words or fewer.

Unit 6 Writing your response    43

## Skills boost

### 2 How do I use evidence to support my ideas?

You can use **key events** in the novel and **key quotations** as evidence to **support** and **explain** your ideas.

Look at one student's **key idea**, or **critical judgement**, in response to this exam-style question.

**Exam-style question**
Starting with this extract, how does Stevenson present tension in *The Strange Case of Dr Jekyll and Mr Hyde*?

The tension and horror are shown in the atmospheric setting. Everything is calm and peaceful until the maid recognises Mr Hyde. Tension builds as she witnesses, but cannot hear, the increasingly impatient encounter between Hyde and Carew, peaking when Hyde clubs Carew to death.

**(1)** Look again at the extract on page 42. Note down **one key event** and **one key quotation** from this point in the novel to support the student's **key idea**.

Key event: ......................................................................................................................................

Key quotation: .................................................................................................................................

**(2)** Now think about **key events** elsewhere in the novel. Which would support the key idea above? Note down **two** key events.

1 ............................................................................  2 ............................................................................

**(3)** Which **key quotations** from the novel would support the key idea above? Tick ✓ any of these.

A  ape-like fury    (Hyde, Chapter 4) ☐

B  It wasn't like a man; it was like some damned Juggernaut.    (Enfield, Chapter 1) ☐

C  'O God!' I screamed, and 'O God!' again and again …    (Lanyon, Chapter 9) ☐

D  … like a monkey jumped from among the chemicals and whipped into the cabinet, it went down my spine like ice.    (Poole, Chapter 8) ☐

E  Dr Jekyll grew pale to the very lips, and there came a blackness about his eyes.    (Chapter 3) ☐

F  'I am ashamed of my long tongue. Let us make a bargain never to refer to this again.'    (Enfield, Chapter 1) ☐

G  fog still slept on the wing above the drowned city …    (Chapter 5) ☐

H  'God bless me, the man seems hardly human! Something troglodytic, shall we say?'    (Utterson, Chapter 2) ☐

I  Think of it – I did not even exist!    (Jekyll, Chapter 10) ☐

J  The mixture, which was at first of a reddish hue, began, in proportion as the crystals melted, to brighten in colour, to effervesce audibly, and to throw off small fumes of vapour.    (Chapter 9) ☐

**(4)** Review the evidence you have gathered above. Which supports the key idea at the top of this page most effectively? ✓

The key events you noted in ②? ☐    The quotations you selected in ③? ☐    or both? ☐

Unit 6 Writing your response

## Skills boost

# 3 How do I analyse my evidence?

Every key **idea** or **point** you make should be supported with **evidence** that you can **analyse**, exploring the effect of the writer's choices of language and structure, what the point suggests about theme and character, and its impact on the reader.

Look at one student's key idea, or **critical judgement**, on the theme of tension in *The Strange Case of Dr Jekyll and Mr Hyde*.

> The tension and horror are shown in the atmospheric setting. Everything is calm and peaceful until the maid recognises Mr Hyde. Tension builds as she witnesses, but cannot hear, the increasingly impatient encounter between Hyde and Carew, peaking when Hyde clubs Carew to death.

Now look at a **key quotation** you could use as evidence to support this key idea.

> And then (all of a sudden) he broke out in a great flame of anger.

To develop an effective analysis, you can consider these **five areas** of analysis:

**A** — Explain the evidence in the context of the whole story: Why does Hyde do this?
*He is unable to stop himself attacking innocent people.*

**B** — Think about language and structure: What does the word 'flame' suggest?
*'Flame' suggests a sudden heat and an unexpected burst of anger.*

**C** — Think about character: What does this suggest about Hyde's character?
*He is unpredictable; he acts suddenly and without warning.*

**D** — Think about theme: What does this suggest about the theme of tension?
*The calm setting and build-up of tension are broken by Hyde's sudden anger and vicious attack.*

**E** — Think about Stevenson's intention: how does the writer want the reader to respond?
*The calm setting and build-up of tension make the attack seem even more shocking and unexpected.*

(1) Look at one student's ideas for analysis of the **key quotation** above. Which ideas would you include in your own analysis of this quote? Tick ✓ them.

(2) Now look at a key event that you could use as evidence to support the key idea above:

> In Chapter 1, Hyde appears out of the darkness and tramples over a young girl.

(3) Use the **five areas of analysis** above to help you note ✎ some ideas you could use in your analysis of this key event. Continue on paper.

Unit 6 Writing your response   45

# Writing your response

**Get back on track**

To write an effective response, you should:
- be familiar with the key events of the novel
- know some key quotations from the novel off by heart
- use key events and key quotations as evidence to support your ideas about the novel's key themes and characters
- analyse your evidence, thinking about language, structure, theme, character and Stevenson's intention.

Look at this exam-style question you saw on page 41.

**Exam-style question**

Starting with this extract, how does Stevenson present tension in *The Strange Case of Dr Jekyll and Mr Hyde*?

Write about:
- how Stevenson presents tension in this extract
- how Stevenson presents tension in the novel as a whole.

Now look at a paragraph focusing on the novel as a whole, taken from one student's response to the question.

> At the end of the story, we see how Stevenson uses tension when Lanyon tells us how he witnesses Hyde turning back into Jekyll. For example, Lanyon builds the tension by telling the story from the beginning, with the arrival of a mysterious man, and then describes his horror at the sight of Hyde's transformation. He recounts how horrified he is and that his mind is 'submerged in terror' at the sight of Hyde changing in front of him. The word 'submerged' suggests that the terror and horror have completely taken over and he can think of nothing else. It also shows how it has shaken his rational view of science. This episode at the end of the novel is the climax of the tension that has been built up through the mysterious character of Hyde, when Stevenson finally lets us see the frightening truth.

- uses a key event as evidence
- uses a quotation as evidence
- explains the context of the evidence
- analysis comments on the writer's choices of language and/or structure
- analysis comments on character
- analysis comments on theme
- analysis comments on Stevenson's intention

(1) Can you identify all the different things the student has included in this paragraph?
Link ✏️ the annotations to the paragraph to show where the student has included them.

# Your turn!

**Get back on track**

You are now going to **write your own answer** in response to the exam-style question.

> **Exam-style question**
>
> Starting with this extract, how does Stevenson present tension in *The Strange Case of Dr Jekyll and Mr Hyde*?
>
> Write about:
> - how Stevenson presents tension in this extract
> - how Stevenson presents tension in the novel as a whole.
>
> (30 marks)

**1** Write ✏ **one** or **two** sentences summarising your critical judgement in response to the question: How is tension presented?

..................................................................................................................................

..................................................................................................................................

**2** Which key events in the novel would support your critical judgement? Note ✏ them below.

**3** Which quotations could you explore in your response? Add ✏ them above.

**4** Look at all the evidence you have gathered. Think about:
- language and structure in your quotations
- what your evidence suggests about the characters
- what your evidence suggests about the theme of tension
- what your evidence suggests about Stevenson's intention: how might the reader respond at this point?

Annotate ✏ your evidence with your ideas.

**5** Look at your annotated evidence.

  **a** Which are your strongest ideas? Tick ✓ them.

  **b** Number ✏ the ideas that you have ticked, sequencing them to build an argument that supports your critical judgement.

**6** Now write ✏ your response to the exam-style question above on paper.

**Unit 6 Writing your response** 47

# Review your skills

### Check up

Review your response to the exam-style question on page 47. Tick ✓ the column to show how well you think you have done each of the following.

|   | Not quite ✓ | Nearly there ✓ | Got it! ✓ |
|---|---|---|---|
| selected relevant key events to support my critical judgement | ☐ | ☐ | ☐ |
| selected relevant key quotations to support my critical judgement | ☐ | ☐ | ☐ |
| analysed my evidence effectively | ☐ | ☐ | ☐ |

Look over all of your work in this unit. Note down the **three** most important things to remember when writing your response.

1. ..................................................................................................
2. ..................................................................................................
3. ..................................................................................................

## Need more practice?

Here is another exam-style question, this time Chapter 1 of *The Strange Case of Dr Jekyll and Mr Hyde* on page 75 (Extract C).

### Exam-style question

Starting with this extract, how does Stevenson present friendship in *The Strange Case of Dr Jekyll and Mr Hyde*?

Write about:
- how Stevenson presents friendship in this extract
- how Stevenson presents friendship in the novel as a whole.

(30 marks)

Write your response to this question.

How confident do you feel about each of these **skills?** Colour in the bars.

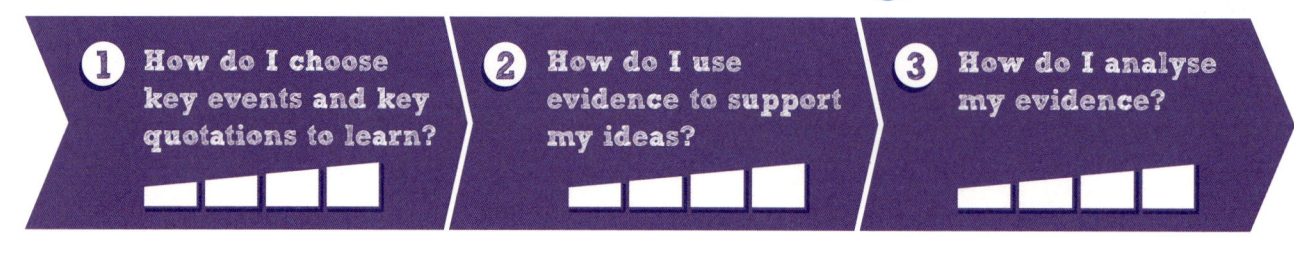

1. How do I choose key events and key quotations to learn?
2. How do I use evidence to support my ideas?
3. How do I analyse my evidence?

48  Unit 6 Writing your response

**Get started**

*Analyse the language, form and structure used by a writer to create meanings and effects (AO2)*

# ⑦ Commenting on structure

This unit will help you to comment on Stevenson's structural choices in *The Strange Case of Dr Jekyll and Mr Hyde*. The skills you will build are to:

- identify significant structural features of the novel
- explore the impact of some of the structural features of the novel, including setting
- build comments on the novel's structure into your analysis.

In the exam you will face a question like the one below. This is about the extract on the next page. At the end of the unit you will **write your own response** to this question.

> **Exam-style question**
>
> Starting with this extract, how does Stevenson present the character of Dr Jekyll in *The Strange Case of Dr Jekyll and Mr Hyde*?
>
> Write about:
> - how Stevenson presents the character of Dr Jekyll in this extract
> - how Stevenson presents the character of Dr Jekyll in the novel as a whole.
>
> (30 marks)

Before you tackle the question you will work through three key questions in the **skills boosts** to help you comment on the settings and structure of the novel.

| ① How can I comment on the settings in the novel? | ② How can I comment on the structure of the novel? | ③ How do I analyse the writer's use of structure? |

Read the extract on the next page from Chapter 5 of *The Strange Case of Dr Jekyll and Mr Hyde*.

### As you read, think about the following: ✓

- What has happened before this extract? What happens after this extract?
- Why has Stevenson chosen to position this conversation at this point in the novel?
- What does the description of Dr Jekyll's house suggest about his position in society in Victorian Britain?

**Unit 7 Commenting on structure** 49

### Get started

> **Exam-style question**
>
> Read the following extract from Chapter 5 of *The Strange Case of Dr Jekyll and Mr Hyde*.
>
> At this point in the novel, Mr Utterson visits Dr Jekyll following the murder of Sir Danvers Carew.

**Extract A | Chapter 5 of *The Strange Case of Dr Jekyll and Mr Hyde***

It was late in the afternoon, when Mr Utterson found his way to Dr Jekyll's door, where he was at once admitted by Poole, and carried down by the kitchen offices and across a yard which had once been a garden, to the building which was indifferently known as the laboratory or dissecting rooms. The doctor had bought the house from the heirs of a celebrated surgeon; and his own tastes being rather chemical than anatomical, had changed the
5  destination of the block at the bottom of the garden. It was the first time that the lawyer had been received in that part of his friend's quarters; and he eyed the dingy, windowless structure with curiosity, and gazed round with a distasteful sense of strangeness as he crossed the theatre, once crowded with eager students and now lying gaunt and silent, the tables laden with chemical apparatus, the floor strewn with crates and littered with packing straw, and the light falling dimly through the foggy cupola. At the further end, a flight of stairs mounted to a door
10  covered with red baize; and through this, Mr Utterson was at last received into the doctor's cabinet. It was a large room fitted round with glass presses, furnished, among other things, with a cheval-glass and a business table, and looking out upon the court by three dusty windows barred with iron. The fire burned in the grate; a lamp was set lighted on the chimney shelf, for even in the houses the fog began to lie thickly; and there, close up to the warmth, sat Dr Jekyll, looking deathly sick. He did not rise to meet his visitor, but held out a cold hand and bade him
15  welcome in a changed voice.
'And now,' said Mr Utterson, as soon as Poole had left them, 'you have heard the news?'
The doctor shuddered. 'They were crying it in the square,' he said. 'I heard them in my dining-room.'
'One word,' said the lawyer. 'Carew was my client, but so are you, and I want to know what I am doing. You have not been mad enough to hide this fellow?'
20  'Utterson, I swear to God,' cried the doctor, 'I swear to God I will never set eyes on him again. I bind my honour to you that I am done with him in this world. It is all at an end. And indeed he does not want my help; you do not know him as I do; he is safe, he is quite safe; mark my words, he will never more be heard of.'
The lawyer listened gloomily; he did not like his friend's feverish manner. 'You seem pretty sure of him,' said he; 'and for your sake, I hope you may be right. If it came to a trial, your name might appear.'

Unit 7 Commenting on structure

## Skills boost

### 1 How can I comment on the settings in the novel?

The settings in *The Strange Case of Dr Jekyll and Mr Hyde* help Stevenson to develop the reader's understanding of his characters and the themes he wants to explore.

1. Look at some key quotations from the extract on page 50. What do they suggest about the setting (Victorian Britain) of the novel?

   > where he was at once admitted by Poole

   > a lamp was set lighted on the chimney shelf, for even in the houses the fog began to lie thickly

   > You seem pretty sure of him,' said he; 'and for your sake, I hope you may be right. If it came to a trial, your name might appear.'

   Write 🖉 **one** or **two** sentences, summing up your ideas.

   ........................................................................
   ........................................................................

2. There is a wide variety of settings within the novel. Each one reflects the character who lives there, or a theme of the novel.

   **A** Hyde's rooms
   > glazed presses full of chemicals | a perfect mat of cobwebs | few dark closets and a spacious cellar

   **B** Streets of London
   > freshly painted shutters, well-polished brasses, and general cleanliness

   **C** Utterson's house
   > his bachelor house | went into his business room | a bottle of a particular old wine that had long dwelt unsunned in the foundations of his house

   **D** Streets of London
   > a dingy street, a gin palace | Tramps slouched into the recess | ragged children huddled in the doorways

   Complete 🖉 the sentences below, thinking about similarities and differences in these settings.

   > Think about:
   > - which theme or character each setting represents
   > - what each setting reveals.

   **a** What do settings B and D tell us about Victorian London?

   ........................................................................
   ........................................................................
   ........................................................................

   **b** What do settings A and C tell us about the characters who live there?

   ........................................................................
   ........................................................................

3. In what ways are all the settings above similar to and different from Jekyll's home? Write 🖉 **one** or **two** sentences explaining your ideas.

   **Jekyll's home**
   > pleasantest room in London | comfortable hall | three dusty windows barred with iron

   ........................................................................
   ........................................................................

Unit 7 Commenting on structure

## Skills boost

### 2 How can I comment on the structure of the novel?

*The Strange Case of Dr Jekyll and Mr Hyde* is structured in 10 chapters. The first eight chapters are written in the third person narrative. Chapters 9 and 10 are letters written by Lanyon and Jekyll in the first person. Stevenson uses this structure to tell the mystery of the novel and then to reveal the truth about the events to the reader from a different perspective.

**1** Think about how Stevenson has structured the novel to manipulate his readers. Add some or all of the words below, and/or some of your own ideas, to the flow chart beneath.

| Jekyll's | good | duality | calmness | Lanyon's | fear | Carew's |
| Hyde's | evil | suffering | isolation | death | violence | transformation |

*You may want to use some words more than once.*

**Beginning: Chapters 1–3**
Stevenson engages the reader's attention with ................

**Middle: Chapters 4–8**
Stevenson holds the reader's attention with ................

**End: Chapters 9 and 10**
Stevenson creates a satisfying ending for the reader with ................

**2** Chapters 1, 4 and 9 are structured around Mr Hyde and the revelation that he is Dr Jekyll.

**Trampling of the girl**
Hyde tramples over the girl; he is portrayed as calm, unfeeling and unnatural.

**Murder of Carew**
Mr Hyde is witnessed beating Sir Danvers Carew to death with a cane.

**Transformation from Hyde to Jekyll**
Hyde takes a potion and transforms back into Dr Jekyll in front of Dr Lanyon.

Use the sentence fragments below to help you summarise what each incident shows the reader.

| The trampling of the girl | The murder of Carew | The transformation from Hyde to Jekyll |
| shows the reader | the results of | the consequences of | the importance of | the contrast of |
| Hyde's | Jekyll's | good | duality | violence | menace | strength | experiments |

52    Unit 7 Commenting on structure

## Skills boost

### 3 How do I analyse the writer's use of structure?

You can build effective comments on structure into your analysis of the novel. Think about how a key event develops or contrasts with other key events, and its impact on the reader.

Look at some sentences taken from one student's response to an exam-style question.

**Exam-style question**

Starting with this extract, how does Stevenson present the character of Dr Jekyll in *The Strange Case of Dr Jekyll and Mr Hyde*?

> Stevenson begins Chapter 3 with Dr Jekyll's refusal to discuss Mr Hyde with Utterson. When the name 'Hyde' is mentioned, Jekyll's personality changes and he becomes pale and there is a 'blackness about his eyes'. This shows that he is unwilling to talk about Mr Hyde with his friend.

**(1)** Now look at some sentences focusing on the novel's structure that could be added to this paragraph.

**A** This reaction shows that, at this point in the novel, Jekyll is afraid of his alter ego, Hyde.

**B** This is a change in mood from the very friendly opening of the chapter with the three friends talking, which tells the reader that Jekyll knows a lot more about Hyde than he is willing to admit.

**C** This reference to 'blackness about his eyes' could be read as Jekyll becoming fearful that his duality and creation of Hyde are about to be found out.

**D** Jekyll's reaction to Utterson shows how easily he can change from being happy to becoming angry and fearful, which mirrors the physical transformation he undergoes in the novel to become Hyde.

**a** Which **two** sentences would you add to the paragraph above to explore the impact of structure? Tick ✓ them.

**b** Mark ✏ where you would add them by writing the letter **A**, **B**, **C**, etc. on the student's response paragraph above.

**(2)** Now look at another paragraph taken from the same student's response.

> Another way in which Stevenson presents Dr Jekyll is through his 'statement' at the end of the novel. This statement is very important to our understanding of the novel and is written from the point of view of Dr Jekyll in the first person. Through this statement, we learn about Dr Jekyll's struggle with his dual nature first-hand and it helps explain all of the events in the novel.

Write ✏ **one** or **two** sentences that could be added to this paragraph, to develop the analysis by focusing on the novel's structure.

You could comment on:
- why and how the letters at the end of the novel are so important
- how the events outlined in Jekyll's statement compare with the events in chapters 1–8.

......................................................................

......................................................................

Unit 7 Commenting on structure 53

# Commenting on structure

**Get back on track**

To comment on the structure of the novel, you need to:
- identify significant structural choices that Stevenson has made
- consider how Stevenson has used these structural choices to manipulate the reader's response to the characters and events in the novel
- link these structural features and their impact to the focus of the question.

Look at this exam-style question you saw at the start of the unit.

### Exam-style question

Starting with this extract, how does Stevenson present the character of Dr Jekyll in *The Strange Case of Dr Jekyll and Mr Hyde*?

Write about:
- how Stevenson presents the character of Dr Jekyll in this extract
- how Stevenson presents the character of Dr Jekyll in the novel as a whole.

Now look at a paragraph taken from one student's response to the question.

> The story of Dr Jekyll and Mr Hyde follows the life of Dr Jekyll as he struggles with his two personalities and the creation of his alter ego, Mr Hyde. In Victorian society, appearance meant everything and we can see how Jekyll goes to great lengths to keep his experiments and his feelings of duality away from his friends. He feels he is unable to admit his long-held beliefs that 'man is not truly one, but truly two'. He lives in a very pleasant and expensive house in a nice part of London and ensures that Mr Hyde leaves and enters through the broken and dirty door on a side street. At the beginning of the novel, we meet the evil Mr Hyde first and Mr Enfield relates the tale of his violent behaviour, and, like Enfield, we are unable to understand who Hyde is and what motivates him. At the end of the novel, we are able to read the very personal statement from Dr Jekyll, where he uses emotive and powerful language to explain why he acted as he did. We are able to understand his motives and his struggles to conform to a conventional life.

1. What is the significant structural choice that the student explores in this paragraph? Underline (A) it and label it **'structure'**.

2. Identify the part of the paragraph in which the student comments on the impact of Stevenson's structural choice. Underline (A) it and label it **'intention'**.

3. Identify the part of the paragraph in which the student links this structural feature and its impact to the focus of the question. Underline (A) it and label it **'question'**.

54     Unit 7 Commenting on structure

# Your turn!

**Get back on track**

You are now going to **write your own answer** in response to the exam-style question.

> **Exam-style question**
>
> Starting with this extract, how does Stevenson present the character of Dr Jekyll in *The Strange Case of Dr Jekyll and Mr Hyde*?
>
> Write about:
> - how Stevenson presents the character of Dr Jekyll in this extract
> - how Stevenson presents the character of Dr Jekyll in the novel as a whole.
>
> (30 marks)

1. Write **one** or **two** sentences summarising your critical judgement in response to the question.

2. Which key events and/or quotations would support your critical judgement?

3. Look at all the evidence you have gathered. Think about how you could use it to comment on:
   - **language** and **structure** in your quotations
   - **character**
   - the **theme** you are exploring: justice and fairness
   - the **structure** of the novel
   - Stevenson's **intention**: how might the reader respond?

   Annotate your evidence with your ideas.

4. Look at your annotated evidence.
   
   a. Which are your strongest ideas? Tick ✓ them.
   
   b. Number the ideas you have ticked, sequencing them to build a response that supports your critical judgement.

5. Now write your response to the exam-style question above on paper.

Unit 7 Commenting on structure    55

# Review your skills

## Check up

Review your response to the exam-style question on page 55. Tick ✓ the column to show how well you think you have done each of the following.

|  | Not quite ✓ | Nearly there ✓ | Got it! ✓ |
|---|---|---|---|
| selected relevant evidence, commenting on character and theme | ☐ | ☐ | ☐ |
| identified relevant and significant structural features of the novel | ☐ | ☐ | ☐ |
| commented on the impact of those structural features | ☐ | ☐ | ☐ |
| linked my comments on structure to the focus of the question | ☐ | ☐ | ☐ |

Look over all of your work in this unit. Note down the **three** most important things to remember when commenting on the structure of the novel.

1. ......................................................................................................................
2. ......................................................................................................................
3. ......................................................................................................................

## Need more practice?

Look at this exam-style question, this time relating to Chapter 2 of *The Strange Case of Dr Jekyll and Mr Hyde* on page 76 (Extract D).

### Exam-style question

Starting with this extract, how does Stevenson present the relationship between Jekyll and Hyde in *The Strange Case of Dr Jekyll and Mr Hyde*?

Write about:
- how Stevenson presents the relationship between Jekyll and Hyde in this extract
- how Stevenson presents the relationship between Jekyll and Hyde in the novel as a whole.

(30 marks)

Plan your response to the question.
- Which key events will you focus on? Note them down.
- Which key structural features of the novel will you focus on? Add them to your plan.
- What impact do these structural features have on the presentation of Jekyll and Hyde in *The Strange Case of Dr Jekyll and Mr Hyde*? Note your ideas.

How confident do you feel about each of these **skills**? Colour in the bars.

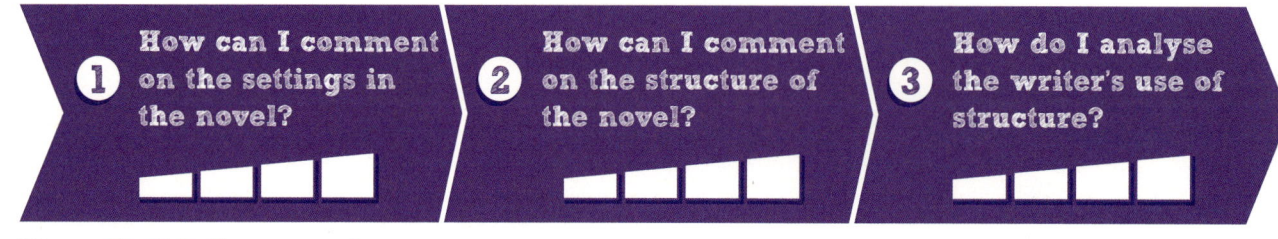

1. How can I comment on the settings in the novel?
2. How can I comment on the structure of the novel?
3. How do I analyse the writer's use of structure?

**Get started**

Show understanding of the relationships between texts and the contexts in which they were written (AO3)

# 8 Commenting on context

This unit will help you to show your understanding of the novel's context: its relationship with the time the novel was written. The skills you will build are to:

- understand the relationship between the novel and its context
- explain the impact of context on different elements of the novel
- incorporate comments on context into your writing about the novel.

In the exam you will face a question like the one below. This is about the extract on the next page. At the end of the unit you will **write your own response** to this question.

**Exam-style question**

Starting with this extract, how does Stevenson present the city of London in *The Strange Case of Dr Jekyll and Mr Hyde*?

Write about:

- how Stevenson presents the city of London in this extract
- how Stevenson presents the city of London in the novel as a whole.

(30 marks)

Before you tackle the question you will work through three key questions in the **skills boosts** to help you write about the novel's context.

1. How do I know which contextual ideas to write about?
2. How do I comment on context?
3. How do I build my comments on context into my analysis?

Read the extract on the next page from Chapter 4 of *The Strange Case of Dr Jekyll and Mr Hyde*.

**As you read, think about the following:**

- What has happened before this extract? What happens after this extract?
- What does the extract suggest about the weather in London?
- What does the extract suggest about the people who live in London?

Unit 8 Commenting on context    57

### Get started

> **Exam-style question**
>
> Read the following extract from Chapter 4 of *The Strange Case of Dr Jekyll and Mr Hyde*.
>
> At this point in the novel, Utterson is travelling through the streets of London to Mr Hyde's house.

**Extract A** | Chapter 4 of *The Strange Case of Dr Jekyll and Mr Hyde*

It was by this time about nine in the morning, and the first fog of the season. A great chocolate-coloured pall lowered over heaven, but the wind was continually charging and routing these embattled vapours; so that as the cab crawled from street to street, Mr Utterson beheld a marvellous number of degrees and hues of twilight; for here it would be dark like the back-end of evening; and there would be a glow of a rich, lurid brown, like the light
5  of some strange conflagration; and here, for a moment, the fog would be quite broken up, and a haggard shaft of daylight would glance in between the swirling wreaths. The dismal quarter of Soho seen under these changing glimpses, with its muddy ways, and slatternly passengers, and its lamps, which had never been extinguished or had been kindled afresh to combat this mournful reinvasion of darkness, seemed, in the lawyer's eyes, like a district of some city in a nightmare. The thoughts of his mind, besides, were of the gloomiest dye; and when he glanced at
10  the companion of his drive, he was conscious of some touch of that terror of the law and the law's officers, which may at times assail the most honest.

As the cab drew up before the address indicated, the fog lifted a little and showed him a dingy street, a gin palace, a low French eating-house, a shop for the retail of penny numbers and twopenny salads, many ragged children huddled in the doorways, and many women of many different nationalities passing out, key in hand, to have a
15  morning glass; and the next moment the fog settled down again upon that part, as brown as umber, and cut him off from his blackguardly surroundings. This was the home of Henry Jekyll's favourite; of a man who was heir to a quarter of a million sterling.

58     Unit 8 Commenting on context

## Skills boost

### 1 How do I know which contextual ideas to write about?

You need to be aware of all the different contexts of *The Strange Case of Dr Jekyll and Mr Hyde* on which you could comment so that you can choose those that are most relevant to the focus of the question.

**(1)** Look at some of the features of the novel and the time in which it was written. Tick ✓ any that are relevant to the novel, and cross ✗ any that are not.

**Victorian London and the Industrial Revolution**
- ☐ London was over-populated and polluted.
- ☐ The fog was caused by all of the soot and smoke, which was produced by coal fires.
- ☐ There was a big divide between the rich and the poor, with the rich owning large houses and the poor living in cramped conditions.
- ☐ With industrialisation, thousands of workers moved from the countryside into towns and cities, leading to overcrowding.
- ☐ There was a huge gap between the rich, who owned the factories, and the poor, who worked in them.

*The Strange Case of Dr Jekyll and Mr Hyde*
- ☐ Written by Stevenson in 1886
- ☐ Became one of the most popular horror stories
- ☐ Set in foggy and atmospheric London

**Science**
- ☐ Charles Darwin published his theory of evolution in 1859, leading to a belief that there was an animal lurking within the evolved human.
- ☐ Many other new theories emerged, such as physiognomy, which argued that a person's nature could be determined by their facial features.

**Religion**
- ☐ The Victorians were very religious and devout.
- ☐ Many people read the Bible at home either to themselves or aloud to others.
- ☐ There was a conflict between religious belief and the new scientific theories that some considered dangerous.

**Gothic literature**
- ☐ Gothic literature developed in the early 18th century and was very popular in the 1900s.
- ☐ It focused on topics of horror and intrigue, with the protagonists often driven to the edge of madness.
- ☐ Stevenson described *The Strange Case of Dr Jekyll and Mr Hyde* as a 'fine bogey tale'.

**Respectability and appearances**
- ☐ A professional class had begun to develop in Victorian society with many doctors, lawyers and other professions becoming well paid and respected.
- ☐ Many Victorians believed that 'well bred' people had to be married and have a family in order to maintain a respectable life.

**(2)** Now think about some of these key events and characters in the novel.

| Jekyll's experiments | Hyde's violent acts | Lanyon's letter | Utterson |

Annotate 🖉 the diagram with these words, using arrows to link them to all the relevant elements of context.

Unit 8 Commenting on context 59

## Skills boost

## 2 How do I comment on context?

An effective comment on context should focus on **when** the novel was written, a **relevant belief**, **attitude** or **situation** at that time and the impact that Stevenson intended to have on his **reader**.

Look at the beginning of one student's paragraph exploring how the city of London is presented in the extract on page 58.

> Throughout the extract, Stevenson emphasises how frightening the city of London can be with the thick fog and lots of different people walking the streets.

**1** Now look at some different students' comments on the context of the novel in this scene.

**A** There were lots of poor people living and working on the streets in those days.

**B** The city of London is presented as foggy and nightmarish, showing that Victorian London had lots of smoke and people due to the Industrial Revolution.

**C** Stevenson presents London as foggy and atmospheric. This Gothic description adds to the mystery of the scene and also highlights the difference between the rich and the poor to the reader.

**a** Which comment does what? Circle Ⓐ or cross out A̶ the letters in the table below.

| Context | Comment |
|---|---|
| Identifies the time in which the novel was written | A  B  C |
| Identifies a relevant belief, attitude or situation at that time | A  B  C |
| Considers Stevenson's intention | A  B  C |
| Considers the impact on readers | A  B  C |

**b** Which of the comments above would you use when writing about how the city of London is presented in the extract. Tick ✓ **one or more**.

**2** Look at these sentences from the beginning of another student's paragraph on the extract about the city in London.

> *Think about why Stevenson might have chosen to include these descriptions.*

> In Chapter 4, Stevenson introduces us to the poor of London by drawing our attention to the ragged children and the women coming out of the gin palaces.

**a** Write ✎ **one** or **two** sentences adding a contextual comment to the paragraph.

..................................................................................................................
..................................................................................................................
..................................................................................................................

**b** Check your comment. Does it achieve all or most of the criteria listed in question ① **a**? Adjust ✎ it as necessary.

60  **Unit 8 Commenting on context**

## Skills boost

### 3 How do I build my comments on context into my analysis?

You do not need to make contextual comments in every paragraph of your response, but you do need to make them relevant to your analysis of the novel.

Look at a paragraph from a student's response, commenting on how Stevenson presents the city of London in Chapter 1 of *The Strange Case of Dr Jekyll and Mr Hyde*.

> In Chapter 1, Stevenson shows the contrast between the rich and the poor of London when Utterson and Enfield go on their walk. First of all, they are in a part of London which is quiet, with well-painted houses and clean streets, but come upon a 'dingy' neighbourhood, where they see Mr Hyde's 'blistered and distained' door, and we are told that tramps and a number of other people spend time in the doorway without anyone telling them to move away.

**(1)** Now look at some sentences you could add to this paragraph.

A | This emphasises to the readers that there are lots of different areas of London.

B | It shows how people do not care about the areas where the poor live.

C | The blistered door and creepy surroundings remind Enfield of an interesting encounter he had with Mr Hyde, who went through that door.

D | It shows the poor of London in rather a negative light but it also highlights their plight and how they were usually asked to move away from the nicer streets.

E | It highlights the difference between the rich and the poor in the 1880s.

F | Stevenson may have intended this scene to show his Victorian readers how easy it was for fortunes to change as the neglected door is right next to the more respectable streets.

G | It highlights to the reader the Victorians' belief in the importance of appearance above everything else.

H | It suggests that, although there was a huge gap between rich and poor in the 1880s, they all had to live together in a large city.

**a** The sentences either comment on the **impact** of the evidence in the paragraph or comment on the novel's **context**. Decide which heading ('Impact' or 'Context') to add above each of the columns of text.

**b** Which comments on context are relevant to which comments on impact? Draw lines linking them.

**c** Which of the sentences above would you include in a paragraph analysing how Stevenson presents the city of London at this point in the novel? Write the sentence order here.

Unit 8 Commenting on context  61

# Get back on track

# Commenting on context

To comment effectively on context, you need to:
- use a relevant contextual point to develop your analysis of a key point, supported by evidence
- explore what this contextual idea adds to your understanding of Stevenson's intention and his readers' response.

Look at this exam-style question you saw at the start of the unit.

### Exam-style question

Starting with this extract, how does Stevenson present the city of London in *The Strange Case of Dr Jekyll and Mr Hyde*?

Write about:
- how Stevenson presents the city of London in this extract
- how Stevenson presents the city of London in the novel as a whole.

**1** Now look at a paragraph focusing on the novel as a whole, taken from one student's response to the question.

> Stevenson uses many different descriptions to present the city of London. One of the most powerful images occurs when Utterson is waiting for Hyde to appear at the doorway. Stevenson describes the noises of the city as a 'low growl' and a 'vast hum', creating a feeling of a busy, almost monstrous, crowded place. This is in direct contrast to Dr Jekyll's house in the next street, which is praised for its 'wealth and comfort'. Victorian London is therefore seen as being busy and crowded but also as a place for the wealthy to live in comfort. By placing the door of Mr Hyde's house in such a busy area and Dr Jekyll's front door in a much wealthier area, Stevenson is highlighting the Victorian obsession with appearances, as Mr Hyde's door is at the back of Dr Jekyll's house – showing the reader that even the most respectable of people have a hidden, darker side.

- uses a key event as evidence
- uses a quotation as evidence
- comments on the impact of the evidence
- identifies a relevant contextual point
- explores Stevenson's intention in the light of this contextual point
- explores the reader's response in the light of this contextual point

Can you identify all the different things the student has included in this paragraph? Link the annotations to the paragraph to show where the student has included them.

62  Unit 8 Commenting on context

# Your turn!

**Get back on track**

You are now going to **write your own answer** in response to the exam-style question.

**Exam-style question**

Starting with this extract, how does Stevenson present the city of London in *The Strange Case of Dr Jekyll and Mr Hyde*?

Write about:
- how Stevenson presents the city of London in this extract
- how Stevenson presents the city of London in the novel as a whole.

(30 marks)

1. Write **one** or **two** sentences, summarising your critical judgement in response to the question: How does Stevenson present the city of London in *The Strange Case of Dr Jekyll and Mr Hyde*?

   ........................................................................

   ........................................................................

2. Which key events in the novel would support your critical judgement? Note them below.

   **Evidence**

3. Look at all the evidence you have gathered. Think about:
   - what your evidence suggests about the city of London
   - what your evidence suggests about Stevenson's intention: how might the reader respond at this point?

   Annotate your evidence with your ideas.

4. Now think about the relevant contextual points you could make in your response. Annotate your evidence with your ideas.

5. Look at your annotated evidence.

   a. Which are your strongest ideas? Tick them.

   b. Number the ideas you have ticked, and sequence them here to build an argument that supports your critical judgement.

6. Now write your response to the exam-style question above on paper.

**Unit 8 Commenting on context** 63

**Get back on track**

# Review your skills

### Check up

Review your response to the exam-style question on page 63. Tick ✓ the column to show how well you think you have done each of the following.

|  | Not quite ✓ | Nearly there ✓ | Got it! ✓ |
|---|---|---|---|
| identified relevant contextual points | ☐ | ☐ | ☐ |
| used relevant contextual points to develop my analysis | ☐ | ☐ | ☐ |
| explored Stevenson's intention and the reader's response in the light of the novel's context | ☐ | ☐ | ☐ |

Look over all of your work in this unit. Note down the **three** most important things to remember when commenting on context.

1. ......................................................................................................................
2. ......................................................................................................................
3. ......................................................................................................................

### Need more practice?

Look at this exam-style question, this time relating to Chapter 9 on page 77 (Extract E).

**Exam-style question**

Starting with this extract, how does Stevenson present the dangers of scientific experiments in *The Strange Case of Dr Jekyll and Mr Hyde*?

Write about:
- how Stevenson presents the dangers of scientific experiments in this extract
- how Stevenson presents the dangers of scientific experiment in the novel as a whole.

(30 marks)

Write your response to this question.
Aim to include at least **two** comments on the novel's context.

How confident do you feel about each of these **skills**? Colour in the bars.

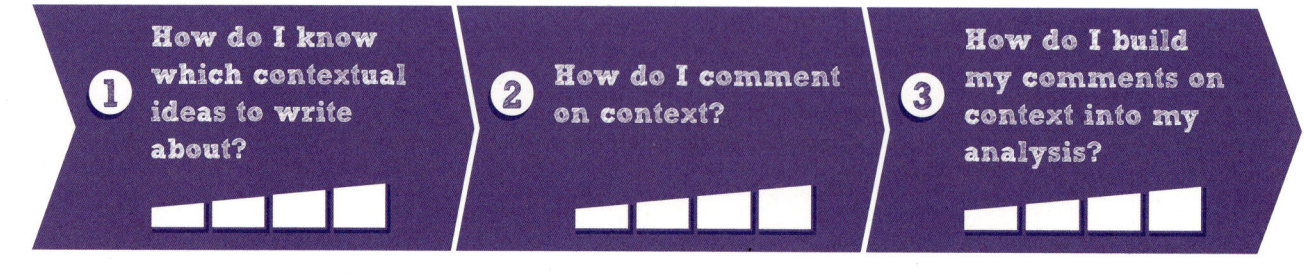

1. How do I know which contextual ideas to write about?
2. How do I comment on context?
3. How do I build my comments on context into my analysis?

**Get started**

Use a range of vocabulary and sentence structures for clarity, purpose and effect (AO4)

# ⑨ Developing a critical writing style

This unit will help you to express your ideas about *The Strange Case of Dr Jekyll and Mr Hyde* as clearly and precisely as possible. The skills you will build are to:

- select vocabulary to express your ideas precisely
- link your ideas to express them clearly
- extend your sentences to develop ideas more fully.

In the exam you will face questions like the one below. This is about the extract on the next page. At the end of the unit you will **write one paragraph** in response to this question.

> **Exam-style question**
>
> Starting with this extract, how does Stevenson present Mr Hyde as unnatural in *The Strange Case of Dr Jekyll and Mr Hyde*?
>
> Write about:
>
> - how Stevenson presents Mr Hyde as unnatural in this extract
> - how Stevenson presents Mr Hyde as unnatural in the novel as a whole.
>
> (30 marks)

Before you tackle the question you will work through three key questions in the **skills boosts** to help you develop a critical writing style.

| ① How do I choose vocabulary that expresses my ideas precisely? | ② How can I link my ideas to express them more clearly? | ③ How can I extend my sentences to develop my ideas more fully? |

Read the extract on the next page from Chapter 10 of *The Strange Case of Dr Jekyll and Mr Hyde*.

**As you read, think about the following:**

- What has happened before this extract? What happens after this extract?
- How does Jekyll's description of Hyde in the extract show he is unnatural?
- How does Jekyll's explanation of Hyde's appearance explain the reasons for his unnatural appearance?

Unit 9 Developing a critical writing style      65

## Get started

> **Exam-style question**
>
> Read the following extract from Chapter 10 of *The Strange Case of Dr Jekyll and Mr Hyde* and then answer the question on page 65.
>
> At this point in the novel, Dr Jekyll explains why he needed to create Mr Hyde.

**Extract A** | Chapter 10 of *The Strange Case of Dr Jekyll and Mr Hyde*

The evil side of my nature, to which I had now transferred the stamping efficacy, was less robust and less developed than the good which I had just deposed. Again, in the course of my life, which had been, after all, nine tenths a life of effort, virtue and control, it had been much less exercised and much less exhausted. And hence, as I think, it came about that Edward Hyde was so much smaller, slighter and younger than Henry Jekyll. Even as good shone
5   upon the countenance of the one, evil was written broadly and plainly on the face of the other. Evil besides (which I must still believe to be the lethal side of man) had left on that body an imprint of deformity and decay. And yet when I looked upon that ugly idol in the glass, I was conscious of no repugnance, rather of a leap of welcome. This, too, was myself. It seemed natural and human. In my eyes it bore a livelier image of the spirit, it seemed more express and single, than the imperfect and divided countenance I had been hitherto accustomed to call mine. And
10  in so far I was doubtless right. I have observed that when I wore the semblance of Edward Hyde, none could come near to me at first without a visible misgiving of the flesh. This, as I take it, was because all human beings, as we meet them, are commingled out of good and evil: and Edward Hyde, alone in the ranks of mankind, was pure evil. I lingered but a moment at the mirror: the second and conclusive experiment had yet to be attempted; it yet remained to be seen if I had lost my identity beyond redemption and must flee before daylight from a house that
15  was no longer mine; and hurrying back to my cabinet, I once more prepared and drank the cup, once more suffered the pangs of dissolution, and came to myself once more with the character, the stature and the face of Henry Jekyll. That night I had come to the fatal cross-roads. Had I approached my discovery in a more noble spirit, had I risked the experiment while under the empire of generous or pious aspirations, all must have been otherwise, and from these agonies of death and birth, I had come forth an angel instead of a fiend. The drug had no discriminating
20  action; it was neither diabolical nor divine; it but shook the doors of the prisonhouse of my disposition; and like the captives of Philippi, that which stood within ran forth. At that time my virtue slumbered; my evil, kept awake by ambition, was alert and swift to seize the occasion; and the thing that was projected was Edward Hyde. Hence, although I had now two characters as well as two appearances, one was wholly evil, and the other was still the old Henry Jekyll, that incongruous compound of whose reformation and improvement I had already learned to despair.
25  The movement was thus wholly toward the worse.

## Skills boost

### 1. How do I choose vocabulary that expresses my ideas precisely?

You need to choose precise vocabulary to describe your response to the novel as fully and accurately as possible.

**(1)** How would you describe Stevenson's presentation of Hyde at **each** of these key points?

Hyde…   ①   ②

**Chapter 1**
- A tramples over a young girl
- B is silent and unapologetic after he is caught
- C is likened to 'Satan' by Enfield

**Chapter 2**
- D appears to Utterson as hardly human

**Chapter 4**
- E witnessed talking to Carew by the maid
- F beats Carew to death with a cane

**Chapter 8**
- G is described as 'a monkey' by Poole
- H dies in Dr Jekyll's laboratory

**Chapter 9**
- I arrives at Lanyon's house and alarms him
- J changes from Mr Hyde to Dr Jekyll in front of Lanyon

Choose **two** words from the list below and write them next to the relevant point in the novel. Aim to choose words that describe your response as precisely as possible. You could choose two words with a similar meaning, or two very different words.

| cold-hearted | terrifying | small | secretive | eerie | sympathetic |
| Devil-like | ugly | hunched | mysterious | unpredictable | dominant |
| unkind | unnatural | uncontrollable | hidden | elusive | vulnerable |
| cruel | unnerving | strong | quiet | unkind | frightening |
| evil | savage | aggressive | uncaring | powerful | desperate |

**(2)** Now think about Stevenson's intention: how did he want readers to respond to Hyde at these points in the novel? Choose **one** or **two** of the words below and add them to each of the key points in the novel in question ①.

| mystery | violence | tension | fear | confusion | disgust | anger | intrigue |
| horror | relief | repulsion | shock | sympathy | concern | surprise | |

Unit 9 Developing a critical writing style   67

## Skills boost

### 2. How can I link my ideas to express them more clearly?

You can use conjunctions to link your ideas, helping you to express your ideas more clearly and fluently.

**Coordinating conjunctions** link related or contrasting ideas:

and | but | or | so

**Subordinating conjunctions** express more complex connections:
- an explanation, e.g. because | in order to
- a comparison, e.g. although | whereas
- a sequence, e.g. when | after | until

**1** Look at these pairs of sentences.

A

☐ Mr Enfield catches Mr Hyde. He is silent and menacing.

☐ Mr Hyde kills Danvers Carew. He is clearly out of control and unpredictable in his behaviour.

☐ Danvers Carew is portrayed as calm and friendly. Hyde is angry and terrifying.

B

☐ After Mr Enfield catches Mr Hyde, he is silent and menacing.

☐ Mr Hyde kills Danvers Carew because Mr Hyde is clearly out of control and unpredictable in his behaviour.

☐ Danvers Carew is portrayed as calm and friendly, whereas Hyde is angry and terrifying.

**a** Circle Ⓐ the **conjunctions** in the sentences labelled B.

**b** Tick ✓ the version of each sentence that you feel is more clearly and fluently expressed.

> Notice that, in some sentences, the conjunction is positioned at the start of the sentence and, in others, in the middle.

**2** Rewrite ✏️ these pairs of sentences, using a conjunction to link them. Remember to choose and position your conjunction carefully to express each idea as clearly and fluently as possible.

| Hyde is monstrous and unpredictable. | + | He savagely beats Danvers Carew to death. |

..................................................................................................................

| Hyde has to transform into Jekyll in front of Lanyon. | + | Lanyon needs to see the truth. |

..................................................................................................................

| Hyde is secretive and hides in the shadows. | + | Utterson is able to approach him outside the door. |

..................................................................................................................

**68** Unit 9 Developing a critical writing style

## Skills boost

### 3 How can I extend my sentences to develop my ideas more fully?

One way to extend your sentences, and develop your ideas, is by using conjunctions. Other ways include:
- using present participles: a verb ending in *–ing*
- using the pronoun *which*.

| Conjunctions | and | but | when | as | before | after |
|---|---|---|---|---|---|---|
| | although | if | whereas | unless | because | since |

You could complete this sentence:

> Hyde is described as being ape-like…

- using this conjunction: → (after) the maid witnesses him beating a man to death.

- or a different conjunction: → (whereas) Utterson describes him as 'hardly human'.

- or a present participle: → (making) the reader see him as strong and aggressive.

- or *which*: → (which) shows that he is unnatural and not like other men.

**1** Complete ✎ this sentence in three different ways.

> Utterson is convinced Mr Hyde is blackmailing Dr Jekyll

a Use a conjunction: ......................................................................................................

b Use a present participle: ......................................................................................................

c Use *which*: ......................................................................................................

You can use *which* or a present participle to avoid repeatedly beginning sentences with 'This suggests…' or 'This shows…'.

For example:

| Hyde is calm after he trampled over the girl. (This suggests) how different he is from other men. | Hyde is calm after he trampled over the girl, (which suggests) how different he is from other men. | Hyde is calm after he trampled over the girl, (suggesting) how different he is from other men. |
|---|---|---|

**2** Change ✎ these sentences to make them a single sentence, using a present participle or *which*.

> Hyde ransacks his rooms after he has killed Carew. This creates the impression that he is escaping and may never be seen again.

> Hyde appears at Dr Lanyon's house. This shows that he is desperate for help and can no longer keep his identity a secret.

Unit 9 Developing a critical writing style

# Developing a critical writing style

**Get back on track**

To express your ideas clearly and precisely, you can:
- select vocabulary that expresses your ideas precisely
- link your ideas using conjunctions, present participles, etc. to develop and express them clearly.

Now look at this exam-style question you saw on page 65.

### Exam-style question

Starting with this extract, how does Stevenson present Mr Hyde as unnatural in *The Strange Case of Dr Jekyll and Mr Hyde*?

Write about:
- how Stevenson presents Mr Hyde as unnatural in this extract
- how Stevenson presents Mr Hyde as unnatural in the novel as a whole.

**1** Look at a short paragraph from one student's response to the question.

> At the start of the novel Hyde is presented as evil. He won't talk after the incident with the girl. He scares Enfield with his appearance. The doctor wants to kill him. Everyone is scared of him but can't say why. This suggests that he is different. It gives the impression that he is a powerful and terrifying man. He is calm and not bothered by what is going on around him.

**a** Underline **at least three** examples of vocabulary which could be more precise.

**b** Note down in the margin **at least three** alternative vocabulary choices for each one.

**c** Highlight any of the sentences which you feel should be linked or developed to improve the clarity and precision of the writing.

**d** Write an improved version of this paragraph, either by adjusting the text above or by rewriting it in the space below.

**Get back on track**

# Your turn!

You are now going to **write one paragraph** in response to the exam-style question.

**Exam-style question**

Starting with this extract, how does Stevenson present Mr Hyde as unnatural in *The Strange Case of Dr Jekyll and Mr Hyde*?

Write about:
- how Stevenson presents Mr Hyde as unnatural in this extract
- how Stevenson presents Mr Hyde as unnatural in the novel as a whole.

(30 marks)

1. a   Think about some of the key events in the novel. Do they show Mr Hyde's personality or his appearance? Which are unnatural? ✓

| Mr Hyde… | Personality | Appearance | Unnatural |
|---|---|---|---|
| • tramples over a young girl | ☐ | ☐ | ☐ |
| • is silent and unapologetic after he is caught | ☐ | ☐ | ☐ |
| • is likened to 'Satan' by Enfield | ☐ | ☐ | ☐ |
| • appears to Utterson as hardly human | ☐ | ☐ | ☐ |
| • is witnessed talking to Carew by the maid | ☐ | ☐ | ☐ |
| • beats Carew to death with a cane | ☐ | ☐ | ☐ |
| • is described as 'a monkey' by Poole | ☐ | ☐ | ☐ |
| • arrives at Lanyon's house and alarms him | ☐ | ☐ | ☐ |
| • changes from Hyde to Jekyll in front of Lanyon | ☐ | ☐ | ☐ |

   b   Choose **one** or **two** of the key events from the novel which you can explore in your response to the exam-style question. Choose from the list above, or use your own ideas. Note them on paper.

   c   Look at each of your chosen events. How is Hyde is presented? How and why is Hyde unnatural? How has Stevenson created that impression? Add them to your notes.

   d   Use your ideas to write one paragraph in response to the exam-style question on paper.

   **Remember:**
   - choose your vocabulary carefully
   - think about ways in which you can link your ideas to develop and express them clearly and precisely.

**Unit 9 Developing a critical writing style**

**Get back on track**

# Review your skills

**Check up**

Review your response to the exam-style question on page 71. Tick the column to show how well you think you have done each of the following.

|  | Not quite | Nearly there | Got it! |
|---|---|---|---|
| selected precise vocabulary | ☐ | ☐ | ☐ |
| linked and developed my ideas clearly and precisely using conjunctions, present participles, etc. | ☐ | ☐ | ☐ |

Look over all of your work in this unit. Note down the **three** most important things to remember when trying to express your ideas as clearly and precisely as possible.

1. ......................................................................................................................
2. ......................................................................................................................
3. ......................................................................................................................

**Need more practice?**

You can EITHER:

**1** Look again at your paragraph written in response to the exam-style question on page 71. Rewrite it, experimenting with different vocabulary choices and sentence structures, linking your ideas in different ways. Which are most effective in expressing your ideas clearly and precisely?

AND/OR:

**2** Choose a **second** point from the suggestions on page 71. Write a further paragraph in response to the exam-style question, focusing closely on your vocabulary choice and sentence structures.

How confident do you feel about each of these **skills?** Colour in the bars.

**1** How do I choose vocabulary that expresses my ideas precisely?

**2** How can I link my ideas to express them more clearly?

**3** How can I extend my sentences to develop my ideas more fully?

72  Unit 9 Developing a critical writing style

# More practice questions

## Units 1 and 2

**Exam-style question**

Read the following extract from Chapter 2 of *The Strange Case of Dr Jekyll and Mr Hyde* and then answer the question that follows.

At this point in the novel, Utterson meets Mr Hyde for the first time.

**Extract A | Chapter 2 of *The Strange Case of Dr Jekyll and Mr Hyde***

'Yes,' returned Mr Hyde, 'It is as well we have met; and apropos, you should have my address.' And he gave a number of a street in Soho.
'Good God!' thought Mr Utterson, 'can he, too, have been thinking of the will?' But he kept his feelings to himself and only grunted in acknowledgment of the address.
5   'And now,' said the other, 'how did you know me?'
'By description,' was the reply.
'Whose description?'
'We have common friends,' said Mr Utterson.
'Common friends,' echoed Mr Hyde, a little hoarsely. 'Who are they?'
10  'Jekyll, for instance,' said the lawyer.
'He never told you,' cried Mr Hyde, with a flush of anger. 'I did not think you would have lied.'
'Come,' said Mr Utterson, 'that is not fitting language.'
The other snarled aloud into a savage laugh; and the next moment, with extraordinary quickness, he had unlocked the door and disappeared into the house.
15  The lawyer stood awhile when Mr Hyde had left him, the picture of disquietude. Then he began slowly to mount the street, pausing every step or two and putting his hand to his brow like a man in mental perplexity. The problem he was thus debating as he walked, was one of a class that is rarely solved. Mr Hyde was pale and dwarfish, he gave an impression of deformity without any nameable malformation, he had a displeasing smile, he had borne himself to the lawyer with a sort of murderous mixture of timidity and boldness, and
20  he spoke with a husky, whispering and somewhat broken voice; all these were points against him, but not all of these together could explain the hitherto unknown disgust, loathing and fear with which Mr Utterson regarded him. 'There must be something else,' said the perplexed gentleman. 'There is something more, if I could find a name for it. God bless me, the man seems hardly human! Something troglodytic, shall we say? or can it be the old story of Dr Fell? or is it the mere radiance of a foul soul that thus transpires through, and
25  transfigures, its clay continent? The last, I think; for, O my poor old Harry Jekyll, if ever I read Satan's signature upon a face, it is on that of your new friend.'

**Unit 1** Starting with this extract, how does Stevenson present Utterson in *The Strange Case of Dr Jekyll and Mr Hyde*?

Write about:

- how Stevenson presents Utterson in this extract
- how Stevenson presents Utterson in the novel as a whole.

(30 marks)

**Unit 2** Starting with this extract, explore how Stevenson presents confrontations in *The Strange Case of Dr Jekyll and Mr Hyde*.

Write about:

- how Stevenson presents the confrontation in this extract
- how Stevenson presents confrontations in the novel as a whole.

(30 marks)

**Unit 1** Which key events in the novel would you choose to write about in your response to this question?

**Unit 2** Write one or two paragraphs in response to this question, focusing on the extract only.

# Units 3 and 4

## Exam-style question

Read the following extract from Chapter 9 of *The Strange Case of Dr Jekyll and Mr Hyde* and then answer the question that follows.

At this point in the novel, Dr Lanyon recounts how Mr Hyde changes into Dr Jekyll.

**Extract B | Chapter 9 of *The Strange Case of Dr Jekyll and Mr Hyde***

He thanked me with a smiling nod, measured out a few minims of the red tincture and added one of the powders. The mixture, which was at first of a reddish hue, began, in proportion as the crystals melted, to brighten in colour, to effervesce audibly, and to throw off small fumes of vapour. Suddenly and at the same moment, the ebullition ceased and the compound changed to a dark purple, which faded again more slowly
5   to a watery green. My visitor, who had watched these metamorphoses with a keen eye, smiled, set down the glass upon the table, and then turned and looked upon me with an air of scrutiny.
'And now,' said he, 'to settle what remains. Will you be wise? will you be guided? will you suffer me to take this glass in my hand and to go forth from your house without further parley? or has the greed of curiosity too much command of you? Think before you answer, for it shall be done as you decide. As you decide, you
10  shall be left as you were before, and neither richer nor wiser, unless the sense of service rendered to a man in mortal distress may be counted as a kind of riches of the soul. Or, if you shall so prefer to choose, a new province of knowledge and new avenues to fame and power shall be laid open to you, here, in this room, upon the instant; and your sight shall be blasted by a prodigy to stagger the unbelief of Satan.'
'Sir,' said I, affecting a coolness that I was far from truly possessing, 'you speak enigmas, and you will perhaps
15  not wonder that I hear you with no very strong impression of belief. But I have gone too far in the way of inexplicable services to pause before I see the end.'
'It is well,' replied my visitor. 'Lanyon, you remember your vows: what follows is under the seal of our profession. And now, you who have so long been bound to the most narrow and material views, you who have denied the virtue of transcendental medicine, you who have derided your superiors – behold!'
20  He put the glass to his lips and drank at one gulp. A cry followed; he reeled, staggered, clutched at the table and held on, staring with injected eyes, gasping with open mouth; and as I looked there came, I thought, a change – he seemed to swell – his face became suddenly black and the features seemed to melt and alter – and the next moment, I had sprung to my feet and leaped back against the wall, my arms raised to shield me from that prodigy, my mind submerged in terror.
25  'O God!' I screamed, and 'O God!' again and again; for there before my eyes – pale and shaken, and half fainting, and groping before him with his hands, like a man restored from death – there stood Henry Jekyll!

**Unit 3** Starting with this extract, how does Stevenson present science and the supernatural in *The Strange Case of Dr Jekyll and Mr Hyde*?

Write about:

- how Stevenson presents science and the supernatural in this extract
- how Stevenson presents science and the supernatural in the novel as a whole.

(30 marks)

**Unit 4** Starting with this extract, how does Stevenson present horrific events in *The Strange Case of Dr Jekyll and Mr Hyde*?

Write about:

- how Stevenson presents horrific events in this extract
- how Stevenson presents horrific events in the novel as a whole.

(30 marks)

**Unit 3** Write **one** or **two** paragraphs in response to this question, focusing on language and structure **in the extract only**.

**Unit 4** Write **two** paragraphs in response to this question, focusing on the second bullet point: **the novel as a whole**.

**More practice questions**

# Units 5 and 6

> **Exam-style question**
>
> Read the following extract from Chapter 1 of *The Strange Case of Dr Jekyll and Mr Hyde* and then answer the question that follows.
>
> At this point in the novel, we are introduced to Mr Utterson, a lawyer.
>
> **Extract C** | Chapter 1 of *The Strange Case of Dr Jekyll and Mr Hyde*
>
> Mr Utterson the lawyer was a man of a rugged countenance that was never lighted by a smile; cold, scanty and embarrassed in discourse; backward in sentiment; lean, long, dusty, dreary and yet somehow lovable. At friendly meetings, and when the wine was to his taste, something eminently human beaconed from his eye; something indeed which never found its way into his talk, but which spoke not only in these silent symbols of
> 5  the after-dinner face, but more often and loudly in the acts of his life. He was austere with himself; drank gin when he was alone, to mortify a taste for vintages; and though he enjoyed the theatre, had not crossed the doors of one for twenty years. But he had an approved tolerance for others; sometimes wondering, almost with envy, at the high pressure of spirits involved in their misdeeds; and in any extremity inclined to help rather than to reprove. 'I incline to Cain's heresy,' he used to say quaintly: 'I let my brother go to the devil in
> 10  his own way.' In this character, it was frequently his fortune to be the last reputable acquaintance and the last good influence in the lives of downgoing men. And to such as these, so long as they came about his chambers, he never marked a shade of change in his demeanour.
> No doubt the feat was easy to Mr Utterson; for he was undemonstrative at the best, and even his friendship seemed to be founded in a similar catholicity of good-nature. It is the mark of a modest man to accept his
> 15  friendly circle ready-made from the hands of opportunity; and that was the lawyer's way. His friends were those of his own blood or those whom he had known the longest; his affections, like ivy, were the growth of time, they implied no aptness in the object. Hence, no doubt the bond that united him to Mr Richard Enfield, his distant kinsman, the well-known man about town. It was a nut to crack for many, what these two could see in each other, or what subject they could find in common. It was reported by those who encountered
> 20  them in their Sunday walks, that they said nothing, looked singularly dull and would hail with obvious relief the appearance of a friend. For all that, the two men put the greatest store by these excursions, counted them the chief jewel of each week, and not only set aside occasions of pleasure, but even resisted the calls of business, that they might enjoy them uninterrupted.

**Unit 5** Starting with this extract, how does Stevenson present Victorian respectability in *The Strange Case of Dr Jekyll and Mr Hyde*?

Write about:

- how Stevenson presents Victorian respectability in this extract
- how Stevenson presents Victorian respectability in the novel as a whole.

(30 marks)

**Unit 6** Starting with this extract, how does Stevenson present friendship in *The Strange Case of Dr Jekyll and Mr Hyde*?

Write about:

- how Stevenson presents friendship in this extract
- how Stevenson presents friendship in the novel as a whole.

(30 marks)

**Unit 5** Plan your response to this question. Aim to:

- sum up your critical judgement in one or two sentences
- identify key events to focus on, and key points to make
- sequence your ideas.

**Unit 6** Write your response to the question.

More practice questions

# Unit 7

> **Exam-style question**
>
> Read the following extract from Chapter 2 of *The Strange Case of Dr Jekyll and Mr Hyde* and then answer the question that follows.
>
> At this point in the novel, Utterson reads Dr Jekyll's will.
>
> **Extract D | Chapter 2 of *The Strange Case of Dr Jekyll and Mr Hyde***
>
> That evening Mr Utterson came home to his bachelor house in sombre spirits and sat down to dinner without relish. It was his custom of a Sunday, when this meal was over, to sit close by the fire, a volume of some dry divinity on his reading desk, until the clock of the neighbouring church rang out the hour of twelve, when he would go soberly and gratefully to bed. On this night however, as soon as the cloth was taken away, he
> 5 took up a candle and went into his business room. There he opened his safe, took from the most private part of it a document endorsed on the envelope as Dr Jekyll's Will and sat down with a clouded brow to study its contents. The will was holograph, for Mr Utterson though he took charge of it now that it was made, had refused to lend the least assistance in the making of it; it provided not only that, in case of the decease of Henry Jekyll, M.D., D.C.L., L.L.D., F.R.S., etc., all his possessions were to pass into the hands of his 'friend and
> 10 benefactor Edward Hyde,' but that in case of Dr Jekyll's 'disappearance or unexplained absence for any period exceeding three calendar months,' the said Edward Hyde should step into the said Henry Jekyll's shoes without further delay and free from any burthen or obligation beyond the payment of a few small sums to the members of the doctor's household. This document had long been the lawyer's eyesore. It offended him both as a lawyer and as a lover of the sane and customary sides of life, to whom the fanciful was the
> 15 immodest. And hitherto it was his ignorance of Mr Hyde that had swelled his indignation; now, by a sudden turn, it was his knowledge. It was already bad enough when the name was but a name of which he could learn no more. It was worse when it began to be clothed upon with detestable attributes; and out of the shifting, insubstantial mists that had so long baffled his eye, there leaped up the sudden, definite presentment of a fiend.
> 20 'I thought it was madness,' he said, as he replaced the obnoxious paper in the safe, 'and now I begin to fear it is disgrace.'
>
> **Unit 7** Starting with this extract, how does Stevenson present the relationship between Jekyll and Hyde in *The Strange Case of Dr Jekyll and Mr Hyde*?
>
> Write about:
> - how Stevenson presents the relationship between Jekyll and Hyde in this extract
> - how Stevenson presents the relationship between Jekyll and Hyde in the novel as a whole.
>
> **(30 marks)**

**Unit 7** Plan your response to the question.
- Which key events will you focus on? Note them down.
- Which key structural features of the novel will you focus on? Add them to your plan.
- What impact do these structural features have on the presentation of Jekyll and Hyde in *The Strange Case of Dr Jekyll and Mr Hyde*? Note your ideas.

# Unit 8

> **Exam-style question**
>
> Read the following extract from Chapter 9 of *The Strange Case of Dr Jekyll and Mr Hyde* and then answer the question that follows.
>
> At this point in the novel, Dr Lanyon looks at the results of Dr Jekyll's experiments.
>
> > **Extract E | Chapter 9 of *The Strange Case of Dr Jekyll and Mr Hyde***
> >
> > Here I proceeded to examine its contents. The powders were neatly enough made up, but not with the nicety of the dispensing chemist; so that it was plain they were of Jekyll's private manufacture: and when I opened one of the wrappers I found what seemed to me a simple crystalline salt of a white colour. The phial, to which I next turned my attention, might have been about half full of a blood-red liquor, which was highly
> > 5  pungent to the sense of smell and seemed to me to contain phosphorus and some volatile ether. At the other ingredients I could make no guess. The book was an ordinary version book and contained little but a series of dates. These covered a period of many years, but I observed that the entries ceased nearly a year ago and quite abruptly. Here and there a brief remark was appended to a date, usually no more than a single word: 'double' occurring perhaps six times in a total of several hundred entries; and once very early in the list and
> > 10 followed by several marks of exclamation, 'total failure!!!' All this, though it whetted my curiosity, told me little that was definite. Here were a phial of some salt, and the record of a series of experiments that had led (like too many of Jekyll's investigations) to no end of practical usefulness. How could the presence of these articles in my house affect either the honour, the sanity, or the life of my flighty colleague? If his messenger could go to one place, why could he not go to another? And even granting some impediment, why was this gentleman
> > 15 to be received by me in secret? The more I reflected the more convinced I grew that I was dealing with a case of cerebral disease; and though I dismissed my servants to bed, I loaded an old revolver, that I might be found in some posture of self-defence.
>
> Starting with this extract, how does Stevenson present the dangers of scientific experiments in *The Strange Case of Dr Jekyll and Mr Hyde*?
>
> Write about:
>
> - how Stevenson presents the dangers of scientific experiments in this extract
> - how Stevenson presents the dangers of scientific experiment in the novel as a whole.
>
> (30 marks)

**Unit 8** Write your response to the question. Aim to include at least **two** comments on the novel's context.

# Answers

## Unit 1

### Page 3

① Twice. Hyde tramples the girl in Chapter 1 and beats Sir Danvers Carew to death in Chapter 4.

② PLUS  ③ b

**Chapters 1–2**
Utterson and Enfield go for a walk and talk about Hyde. Utterson looks at Jekyll's will and finds Hyde is in it. He talks to Dr Lanyon and then meets Hyde in person.

⬇

**Chapters 3–5**
The maid witnesses Hyde murdering Carew. Utterson goes with Inspector Newcomen to Hyde's house. His landlady lets them in.
Utterson reads Hyde's letter with Mr Guest, who thinks the handwriting is very similar to Jekyll's.

⬇

**Chapters 6 and 7**
Lanyon falls ill and dies, leaving a letter for Utterson.

⬇

**Chapters 8 and 9**
Poole wakes Utterson and they break down the door to Jekyll's laboratory with Bradshaw.
Hyde is found dead on the floor. Jekyll is missing. Utterson finds his latest will and a statement to read.
Lanyon's letter reveals that Hyde turned into Jekyll when he drank a potion.

⬇

**Chapter 10**
Jekyll's statement explains why and how he turned into Hyde.

③ a  D Mr Richard Enfield, Dr Hastie Lanyon, Mr Gabriel Utterson, Mr Poole, Dr Henry Jekyll, Mr Edward Hyde

K The maid, Sir Danvers Carew, Inspector Newcomen, Mr Hyde's landlady, Mr Guest, Bradshaw

### Page 4

① a and b

| | |
|---|---|
| Ch. 1 | Mr Utterson and his friend Mr Enfield see a worn doorway. |
| | The door reminds Enfield of a man, Mr Hyde, whom he saw trampling over a girl. He later saw Hyde enter this door, which is at the back of Jekyll's house. |
| Ch. 2 | Utterson reads Dr Jekyll's will, which states that he wants to leave Hyde all his money if he dies or goes missing. |
| | Utterson meets Hyde near the same door and finds him very unnerving. |
| Ch. 4 | A year later, Hyde is witnessed murdering Sir Danvers Carew, an MP. |
| Ch. 5 | Utterson visits an ill Jekyll, who gives him a letter written by Hyde. |
| Ch. 6 | Lanyon falls ill after a terrible shock and dies, leaving a letter for Utterson to read if Jekyll goes missing or dies. |
| Ch. 7 | Enfield and Utterson see an ill Jekyll at the window; he turns away from them. |
| Ch. 8 | Poole asks Utterson to help him break into Jekyll's laboratory, where they discover Hyde, who has killed himself with poison. |
| | There is no sign of Jekyll, but they find a long statement written by him, and a new will, in which he leaves all his money to Utterson. |
| Ch. 9 | Lanyon recounts, in a letter, how Hyde turned into Jekyll in front of him after drinking a potion. |
| Ch. 10 | Jekyll explains in his statement that transforming into Hyde allowed him to live a double life, and how it would lead to his death. |

### Page 5

② b  Possible answers for the three events that are most significant:
- Enfield recounts the tale of a strange man called Mr Hyde. If Enfield had not seen this event, Utterson would not have heard the name and connected it to his friend and the will.
- A year later, Hyde is witnessed murdering a man. If the maid had not seen this and if Carew had not had the letter on him, Hyde might have got away with the whole thing.
- Lanyon's letter recounting how Hyde turned into Jekyll in front of him after drinking a potion confirms our suspicions and reveals all of the clues within the novel that Hyde was the alter ego of Jekyll.

### Page 6

①

| | |
|---|---|
| **Before this extract:** We meet Utterson. He and Enfield are friends but have little in common. Enfield tells him about Hyde and the girl, which reminds Utterson of Jekyll and his will.<br>**After this extract:** Utterson supports Jekyll and receives letters from both Lanyon and Jekyll, which lead him to the truth about Hyde. | Shows awareness of **where** in the novel the extract is taken from |

78  Answers

| So in Chapter 2, the relationship is important, as it introduces us to Hyde through the conversation of the two friends. | Makes a clear, direct **response** to the question. |
|---|---|
| the relationship is important | Uses **key words** from the question. |
| e.g. he has not seen him for 'more than ten years' due to Jekyll's 'unscientific balderdash' | Makes a **range of points** |
| | Supports points with **evidence** |
| e.g. 'unscientific balderdash' – introduces the idea of Jekyll's unconventional ideas about science | **Comments** on the significance of the writer's choices |

## Page 7

1. a) Different relationships: Utterson and Enfield (Chapter 1); Utterson and Lanyon (Chapter 6); Lanyon and Jekyll (Chapters 6, 9); Jekyll and Utterson (Chapters 2, 3, 5, 7, 8).

   b) Importance of relationships:
   - The friendship between Utterson and Enfield introduces us to the story of Hyde.
   - Lanyon's friendship with Utterson means that he leaves the key letter with Utterson.
   - Jekyll turns to Lanyon for help when he is struggling to keep his two personas separate.
   - Jekyll's friendship with Utterson means that the truth is finally revealed and also links Jekyll and Hyde together from the beginning via the will.

# Unit 2

## Page 11

1. a) 2, 5, 6.

   b) Examples include:

      A: Section 2 describes the evil act Mr Hyde commits when he tramples over the girl.

      B: Section 5 describes Mr Enfield's and the doctor's reaction to Mr Hyde's evil look and his cold, calm manner.

      C: Section 6 shows how the crowd dislike Hyde and how he reacts by sneering and appearing to be like 'Satan'.

## Page 12

1. a) Mr Hyde is 'calm' even though he has 'trampled' over a screaming girl. He is not like a man, but like a 'Juggernaut' and he does not stop to help the girl.

   b) Mr Hyde is not like any ordinary man either in his personality or his actions.

   c/d) It reflects, and adds to, the reader's impression of his character. He is 'stumping' along, which is menacing. His action of trampling over the girl and leaving her 'screaming on the ground' shows that he is evil.

2. Hyde gives Enfield a menacing look which is so 'ugly' it causes Enfield to sweat. The doctor is so unnerved that he is desperate to kill Hyde. The people in the crowd become so enraged they have to be held back. Hyde reacts to this all in a sneering manner and gives the impression of being like 'Satan'.

## Page 13

1. a) All are valid.

   b) For example: A, B, E, C, D, F

2. For example:

   [A] The description of Mr Hyde walking over the girl and not looking back develops the reader's impression that he is evil and menacing.

   For example, [B] We are told that he 'trampled over the child's body' and then he left her 'screaming on the ground'.

   This suggests that [E] Instead of being sorry, Hyde is cold and calm at all times.

   In this way, [C] Stevenson describes how Hyde 'wasn't like a man' but like a 'Juggernaut', indicating that he is menacing.

   Similarly, [D] the reactions of others underline his menacing nature, as when Enfield takes a 'loathing' to him, and the look Hyde gives him is so 'ugly' that it makes him sweat.

   It implies that [F] Hyde is evil and not like other people.

3. a) Key point: A
   b) Evidence: B, C, D, E
   c) Comment: C
   d) Response: D

## Page 14

1. a) The student has achieved all of the criteria.

   B Key point: *In this extract, Mr Hyde is clearly shown as evil and menacing.*

   C Evidence: *His actions make this clear to the reader when we are told that he 'calmly trampled over the child's body and left her screaming on the ground'.*

   D Comment: *... implies that Hyde did not care about the screaming girl, which makes him an evil character.*

   C Evidence: *Enfield says Hyde gave him 'one look, so ugly' that it brought him out in a sweat 'like running'.*

   E Response: *The impression created by this sentence is that Hyde is so menacing that he causes other people to be nervous and feel uncomfortable.*

# Unit 3

## Page 19

1. a) For example:
   - 'and flecked the blood into the face'
   - 'never seen that part of London so deserted.'

   b) For example:
   - 'blood'
   - 'deserted'

   c) For example: 'Flecked the blood into the face' suggests a biting wind that makes the blood in your face run cold, which adds to the mystery of the journey; 'London so deserted' gives the empty London streets a sense of mystery as this is not what Utterson is used to.

2. A: a) The weather is used to heighten the air of mystery.

**Answers** 79

- **b/c** The 'wind' and the 'dust' add to the extreme circumstances and the feeling that this is a mysterious situation.
- B: **a** Poole is worried and concerned about what is about to happen.
- **b/c** Poole is sweating despite the cold due to 'strangling anguish', his face is 'white' and his voice is 'broken'.

## Page 20

**1** All are valid. The section shows the servants' confusion as they are not sure who is at the door. Poole is annoyed as they do not open the door straight away. The servants are very relieved to see Utterson and are scared as they have had the door locked and are 'huddled' together.

**2 a** A For example: 'The hall, when they entered it, was brightly lighted up; the fire was built high; and about the hearth the whole of the servants, men and women, stood huddled together like a flock of sheep.'

B For example: 'Open the door.'

C For example: 'Is that you, Poole?'

D For example: 'Bless God!'

**b** For example:
- In Sentence A, Stevenson suggests an air of mystery as at first, the hall seems warm and welcoming but the servants are huddled and scared.
- In Sentence B, Stevenson suggests that Poole is scared as he is curt and brisk with the person who will not open the door.
- In Sentence C, Stevenson suggests a sense of mystery as the servants ask who is knocking at the door and need to check it is Poole.
- In Sentence D, Stevenson uses the exclamation to show the relief of the servants and how they trust Mr Utterson to help them. It acts as a release from the mystery and tension.

**c** For example:
- In Sentence A, Stevenson uses a long sentence to show the change in mood.
- In Sentence C, Stevenson uses a question to show that the servants are scared about what is happening.
- In Sentence D, Stevenson uses an exclamation to highlight the relief of the servants as the appearance of Utterson relieves the sense of mystery.

## Page 21

**1** All are valid.

**2** Comments are likely to focus on:
- the repeated use of the exclamation 'foul play' and how this creates mystery, as Utterson and the reader do not know what has happened.
- the use of the phrase 'a good deal frightened', indicating that Utterson is afraid about this mysterious incident.
- the use of rhetorical questions to heighten the mystery as we follow Utterson's train of thought.

## Page 22

Responses could focus on:

| | |
|---|---|
| key point focusing on the key words in the question | • Stevenson presents a sense of mystery when Poole comes to Utterson's house. |
| evidence from the text to support the point | • 'foul play'<br>• Utterson has a 'crushing anticipation of calamity' and Poole is experiencing 'strangling anguish'. |
| comments on the evidence and its impact | • The repetition of the short exclamation 'foul play' invites the reader to be concerned about what is about to be revealed.<br>• By using long sentences, which slow the pace and build a sense of dread, to describe Utterson's inner thoughts, the mystery is built up and we are expecting the worst when Poole and Utterson arrive at the house. |
| a response to the question. | • Utterson then walks with Poole to Jekyll's laboratory and the weather and atmosphere help to intensify the sense of mystery |
| comments on Stevenson's language choice(s) | • The mysteriousness of the situation is then further underlined by the use of religious language such as 'Amen' and the exclamation – 'Bless God!' as everyone prays for the best<br>• By the time they get there, Utterson has a 'crushing anticipation of calamity' and Poole is experiencing 'strangling anguish'. By using the verbs 'crushing' and 'strangling', Stevenson builds the mystery as we can feel the tension impacting on the characters. |
| comments on Stevenson's choice(s) of structure or sentence form | • The repetition of the short exclamation 'foul play' invites the reader to be concerned about what is about to be revealed.<br>• By using long sentences, which slow the pace and build a sense of dread, to describe Utterson's inner thoughts, the mystery is built up and we are expecting the worst when Poole and Utterson arrive at the house. |

# Unit 4

## Page 27

**1** For example: mysterious, respectable, unconventional, secretive.

**2** For example: conflicted, unhappy, desperate, helpless.

**3** All responses are acceptable. All events show how Dr Jekyll struggles with his alter ego, Mr Hyde, until Mr Hyde takes over completely.

## Page 28

1. 
- duality of human nature: for example, in Chapter 10 Dr Jekyll explains his motivations for becoming Mr Hyde.
- science: for example, in Chapter 2 Dr Lanyon tells Utterson how he and Dr Jekyll have argued about their approaches to science.
- secrets: for example, in Chapter 6 Dr Jekyll's letter to Utterson and why he must retreat from society.
- appearance and reality: for example, the interior and exterior settings of London.

2. Both positive and negative: both Dr Lanyon and Dr Jekyll are well regarded but represent different sides of scientific research. Dr Lanyon is practical and rational, whereas Dr Jekyll highlights the powers that science has. Science helps to explain exactly how Mr Hyde is created but the potion Dr Jekyll creates is both dangerous and deadly.

3. 
   a. For example: the revelation of the dual personality of Dr Jekyll and Mr Hyde; the evil acts of Mr Hyde against the innocent girl and Sir Danvers Carew; the goodness of Dr Jekyll compared with the evil of Mr Hyde.
   b. For example: through the first-person narratives of Dr Jekyll and Dr Lanyon; the settings in Dr Jekyll's house with his hall and his laboratory; the descriptions of the horrific acts of Mr Hyde and the defencelessness of his victims.

## Page 29

1. 
   a. A, D, F, G
   b. B, C, E
   c. For example: Dr Jekyll's changing state of mind keeps the reader in the dark about his true personality. We feel sorry for him as we believe he is being blackmailed and harassed by Mr Hyde, then we are puzzled by his changing moods and treatment of his friends. We are then sympathetic/appalled at the end when we discover that his scientific experiments have led to his physically creating a whole new persona to match the dual feelings he has.

2. 
   a. All could apply.
   b. For example: The presentation of horror shocks the reader, as the descriptions of Hyde turning into Jekyll are quite graphic and show that experimenting with science and potions can be dangerous. The tension and action of the novel are increased by these horrific scenes, causing a final shock to the reader after a lot of scene-setting and build-up. Stevenson's descriptions of the attacks are often detailed, with descriptions about the injuries or the reactions to the events, which may shock the reader.

## Page 30

1. 
   a. For example: Chapter 6, Dr Jekyll is out in public and then retreats into his house; Chapter 9, Mr Hyde transforms into Dr Jekyll.
   b. For example: Paragraph 1, contrasting the actions of Dr Jekyll and his changing moods; Paragraph 2, the man takes a potion and transforms into Dr Jekyll.
   c. This contrast shows how Stevenson firstly shows the different natures of Dr Jekyll; the second paragraph shows how he builds on this by revealing that Jekyll and Hyde are the same person.

## Unit 5

### Page 35

1. 
   a. For example: Lanyon refuses to speak about the incident with Jekyll. He says that Utterson may find out when he is dead but 'I cannot tell you'. He is determined not to speak of it and states how Utterson will have to go if he 'cannot keep clear of this accursed topic'. Jekyll never wants to see Lanyon or Utterson and states how his door will 'often shut even to you'.
   b. For example: Secrets are presented as something that should never be told until after death. They are also something that can never be spoken about as they are too upsetting or they cause a person to be shut away from their friends. They are avoided and have a very negative impact on the mental health of Lanyon and Jekyll.

### Page 36

1. 
   a. All are arguably valid.
   b. Agreements are likely to be:
      Chapter 1 a and b: C, D and E
      Chapter 2 a: B
      Chapter 2 b: A, B
      Chapter 5 a: A, C, D, E,
      Chapter 5 b: C, D, E
      Chapter 8 a: A, D, E
      Chapter 8 b: B, D

2. Key points are likely to focus on how Utterson keeps secrets to protect Dr Jekyll's reputation, and how the gradual revealing of Jekyll's mysterious experiments and the identity of Hyde ensure that the plot moves along.

### Page 37

1. A, B, D, C

2. 
   a. For example, A, C, D, B – through the character of Utterson as he is suspicious of Hyde, then locks up the letter to protect Jekyll. Lanyon and Poole both reveal their secrets about Jekyll to him.
   b. For example, C, B, A, D – focusing first on the letters of Jekyll and Lanyon, followed by the odd behaviour of Jekyll.

### Page 38

Sample response:

1. Utterson keeps secrets to protect his friend; Jekyll keeps Hyde secret to protect his reputation; Lanyon refuses to tell anyone Jekyll's secret as he is too horrified and appalled at the truth; Stevenson uses secrets as a way to build tension and mystery.

2. 
- In chapter 1, Utterson and Enfield believe that Jekyll is being blackmailed
- In chapter 3, Stevenson creates the secretive, mysterious doctor

**answers** 81

- Lanyon keeps Jekyll's secrets, as he is horrified and scared
- Stevenson ensures that we as readers do not find out the truth until Lanyon's letter in chapter 9, which builds the suspense as we do not know why Lanyon is so desperate to keep the secret until that point.

## Unit 6

### Page 43

1. Characters: Hyde, Carew.
   Themes: Horror, Violence, and Good and Evil.

2. a  A Utterson
      B Hyde, Utterson
      C Utterson
      D Hyde
   b  B Violence
      C Atmosphere, Victorian London
      D Appearances and reality
   c  A and D are the most significant.

3. a  All are valid. However, B and D are also relevant to key themes. B shows the transformation from Hyde into Jekyll in front of Lanyon and how Stevenson builds the tension with the use of horror. D shows tension and horror as Jekyll explains that everyone has a dual nature.
   b  For example, 'Like a monkey' (C) and 'not truly one, but truly two' (D).

### Page 44

1. For example, the maid is daydreaming: 'the early part of the night was cloudless, and the lane, which the maid's window overlooked, was brilliantly lit by the full moon.'

2. For example: Hyde is unnerving and terrifies everyone he meets; Utterson witnesses the personality changes in Dr Jekyll and is concerned/confused by them.

3. A, B, C, G, H, I and J are all valid choices.

4. Using both key events and quotations is likely to be a more effective approach.

### Page 45

1, 2  All are valid.

3. For example, Hyde is unthinking and out of control. The word 'tramples' shows that he is aggressive and angry. There is tension as Enfield describes how the girl and Hyde are heading towards each other and then he describes the horror of the scene. Stevenson means to show, at the very start of his novel, that Hyde is a monstrous man who is behaving in an unpredictable way.

### Page 46

Suggestions include:

| uses a key event as evidence | Lanyon tells us how he witnesses Hyde turning back into Jekyll. |
| uses a quotation as evidence | 'submerged in terror' |
| explains the context of the evidence | This episode at the end of the novel is the climax of the tension that has been built up through the mysterious character of Hyde |
| analysis comments on the writer's choices of language and/or structure | The word 'submerged' suggests that the terror and horror have completely taken over and he can think of nothing else |
| analysis comments on character | It also shows how it has shaken his rational view of science. |
| analysis comments on theme | For example, Lanyon builds the tension by telling the story from the beginning, with the arrival of a mysterious man, and then describes his horror at the sight of Hyde's transformation. |
| analysis comments on Stevenson's intention | through the mysterious character of Hyde, when Stevenson finally lets us see the frightening truth. |

## Unit 7

### Page 51

1. 
   - Utterson is admitted into the house by Poole – a butler – showing that the rich have 'staff'.
   - Utterson is concerned in case Jekyll's name should come up in court; this reveals how the society of the time worried about respectability and reputation.
   - The fog was something that pervaded all of Victorian London.

2. a  That there are two different areas reflecting the wealthy in B and the poor and destitute in D.
   b  Utterson lives alone and works in his house. He enjoys his home comforts and has a wine cellar. Hyde's home has chemicals and a lot of unused/unloved rooms. He lives for his scientific work.

3. Jekyll's house is similar to Utterson's house and the rich streets of London and also (as Hyde's rooms are within it) there are some indications that some of the house is unloved/unused.

### Page 52

1. Examples might include these.
   - Beginning: Hyde's evil, calmness, violence
   - Middle: Jekyll's duality, good, isolation, suffering, fear; Hyde's violence, Carew's death; Hyde's death, Lanyon's fear and death
   - End: Hyde's transformation; Lanyon's fear; Jekyll's duality; Jekyll's death

2. Examples might include:
   - The trampling of the girl shows the reader the importance of Hyde's menace and strength.
   - The murder of Carew shows the reader the consequences of Jekyll's duality.
   - The transformation from Hyde to Jekyll shows the reader the results of Jekyll's experiments.

### Page 53

1. a  All are valid, although A is a weaker comment without the support of B and C to develop it.

2. Comments are likely to focus on:
   - the contrast between Dr Jekyll's confident and happy behaviour in Chapters 3 and 5 and Chapter 6 when he appears terrified at the window.

- the shocking consequences of Jekyll's feeling of duality and how his experiments to turn into Hyde cause most of the events in the novel.

## Page 54
Sample responses:

1. The positioning of the appearance of Hyde at the beginning of the story.
2. At the end of the novel we are able to read the very personal statement from Dr Jekyll, where he uses emotive and powerful language to explain why he acted as he did. We are also able to understand his motives and his struggles to conform to a conventional life.
3. He lives in a very pleasant and expensive house in a nice part of London and ensures that Mr Hyde leaves and enters through the broken and dirty door on a side street.

| comments on the impact of the evidence | creating a feeling of a busy, almost monstrous, crowded place |
|---|---|
| identifies a relevant contextual point | Victorian London is therefore seen as being busy and crowded but also as a place for the wealthy to live in comfort. |
| explores Stevenson's intention in the light of this contextual point | Stevenson is highlighting the Victorian obsession with appearances, as Mr Hyde's door is at the back of Dr Jekyll's house – |
| explores the reader's response in the light of this contextual point | showing the reader that even the most respectable of people have a hidden, darker side. |

# Unit 8

## Page 59
1. The Industrial Revolution is less relevant.
2. 
   - Jekyll's experiments: Science; Respectability and appearances; Gothic literature; Religion
   - Hyde's violent acts: Science, Victorian London; Gothic literature
   - Lanyon's letter: Science, Victorian London; Respectability and appearances; Gothic literature
   - Utterson: Victorian London; Religion; Respectability and appearances

## Page 60
1. a) A: Identifies the time in which the novel was written; identifies the situation at that time.
   
   B: Identifies the time in which the novel was written; identifies a relevant situation at that time.
   
   C: Identifies a relevant attitude for the time in which the novel was written; considers Stevenson's intention and its impact on the reader; identifies the time in which the novel was written.
   
   b) B and C are the most detailed, developed comments on context.

2. a) Responses could include, for example:
   
   Stevenson was highlighting the poor of the city by describing their meals and their plight as they are out on the cold streets early in the morning. He also mentions the prostitutes who frequented a number of London streets, as well as the gin palaces, which were popular at the time.

## Page 61
1. a) Sentences A–D focus on impact; sentences E–H focus on context.
   
   b) A–E; B–F, C–G; D–H.

## Page 62
Sample response:

| uses a key event as evidence | One of the most powerful images occurs when Utterson is waiting for Hyde to appear at the doorway. |
|---|---|
| uses a quotation as evidence | Stevenson describes the noises of the city as a 'low growl' and a 'vast hum'. |

# Unit 9

## Page 67
1. For example:
   
   A cruel, evil, uncontrollable, unkind
   
   B frightening, mysterious, unnerving, cold-hearted, quiet
   
   C Devil-like, evil, terrifying
   
   D eerie, unnerving, savage
   
   E mysterious, unnatural
   
   F uncontrollable, evil, cruel
   
   G unnatural, hunched, small
   
   H vulnerable, sympathetic
   
   I vulnerable, frightening, mysterious, desperate
   
   J unnerving, unnatural, mysterious

2. For example:
   
   A surprise, disgust
   
   B confusion, anger, concern
   
   C mystery, horror, intrigue
   
   D confusion, intrigue, tension
   
   E intrigue, tension
   
   F anger, shock, confusion
   
   G confusion, concern, mystery
   
   H relief, concern
   
   I sympathy, fear, intrigue, mystery
   
   J horror, surprise, fear, repulsion

## Page 68
1. a) after, because, whereas
   
   b) All version 'B's use conjunctions to express the relationship between the two clauses more clearly.

2. For example:
   - Hyde is monstrous and unpredictable <u>when</u> he savagely beats Danvers Carew to death.
   - Hyde has to transform into Jekyll in front of Lanyon <u>because</u> Lanyon needs to see the truth.
   - Hyde is secretive and hides in the shadows, <u>although</u> Utterson is able to approach him outside the door.

Answers 83

## Page 69

**1** For example:

- **a** Utterson is convinced Mr Hyde is blackmailing Dr Jekyll when he hears about the cheque Hyde produced with Dr Jekyll's name on it.
- **b** Utterson is convinced Mr Hyde is blackmailing Dr Jekyll, making him go home and re-read Dr Jekyll's mysterious will.
- **c** Utterson is convinced Mr Hyde is blackmailing Dr Jekyll, which shocks him so much that he wonders what secrets Jekyll is hiding.

**2 a** Hyde ransacks his rooms after he has killed Carew, <u>creating</u> the impression the impression that he is escaping and may never be seen again.

- **b** Hyde appears at Dr Lanyon's house, <u>showing</u> that he is desperate for help and can no longer keep his identity a secret.

## Page 70

Sample response:

**1 a/b** e.g. evil (menacing, savage), won't talk, scares (is silent; terrifies, unnerves)

**c/d** e.g.

At the start of the novel Hyde is presented as <u>menacing</u> and <u>savage</u>. He <u>remains silent</u> after the incident with the girl, and <u>unnerves</u> Enfield with his appearance. The doctor wants to kill him, <u>while</u> everyone is scared of him but cannot <u>understand</u> why. This suggests that Hyde is different, <u>giving</u> the impression that he is a powerful and terrifying man, <u>because</u> he is calm and <u>unaffected</u> by the <u>violence</u> around him.